Wisdom FOR Grandparents

Practical Bible-Based Principles

Christian Parenting

Compiled by Gary Wilde

All Scripture quotations, unless indicated, are from the Holy Bible, New International Version ®. Copyright ©1973, 1978, 1984, by International Bible Society. Used by permission of Zondervan Publishing House. All rights reserved.

Christian Parenting Books™ is an imprint of Chariot Family Publishing
Cook Communications Ministries, Elgin, Illinois 60120
Cook Communications Ministries, Paris, Ontario
Kingsway Communications, Eastbourne, England

Cover design by Foster Design Associates
Interior Design by Nancy Haskins
First printing, 1995
Printed in the United States of America
99 98 97 96 95   5 4 3 2 1

♦ Table of Contents ♦

You Do Have Wisdom to Bequeath
Remind Your Grandchildren Not to Forget Their Creator
Biblical Values to Teach Your Grandchildren

- ♦ Compassion
- ♦ Faith
- ♦ Wisdom
- ♦ Obedience to God
- ♦ Forgiveness
- ♦ Honesty
- ♦ Humility
- ♦ Peacefulness
- ♦ Thoughtfulness
- ♦ Happiness

Teach Your Grandchildren, by Word and Example . . .

- ♦ To Avoid Bad Advice and Bad Company
- ♦ To Accept Correction and Discipline for Their Benefits
- ♦ To Appreciate Parental Guidance
- ♦ To Handle Money Wisely
- ♦ To Recognize the Value of Hard Work

♦ Chapter 1 ♦

How can I maintain the joy of living as I get older?

A lot of people think getting older is something negative, something to be feared, or at least avoided in conversation," said Jesse. "But I've found there is so much that is good about this stage of my life: just having more time to pay attention to things, for one. No more hectic pace. The chance to think, pray, praise. I'm always finding new blessings to be thankful for—the little things that used to go unnoticed.

"So one of the best parts of my life right now is taking time to count my blessings. I think about God's care in the past and look for His goodness in the future. Also, I can enjoy the strength and enthusiasm of youth when I watch my grandchildren. I may not always be a 'player' now, but I get a lot of satisfaction out of being a spectator!"

For Memory:
Young men and maidens, old men and children.
Let them praise the name of the LORD,
for his name alone is exalted;
his splendor is above the earth and the heavens.
-Psalm 148:12-13

For Silent Reflection:

♦ *When I think about God's provision in the past, what special instances of goodness and grace come to mind?*

♦ *What forms of blessing from God do I expect to enjoy in my future?*

♦ *How hard or easy is it for me to take pleasure in the energy of children? What can I do to enhance my joy in this area?*

♦ *What are the most rewarding and pleasant aspects of grandparenting for me? The most challenging or difficult?*

Be Thankful: God Has Blessed You over the Years!

Sons are a heritage from the LORD,
children a reward from him. *-Psalm 127:3*

Our mouths were filled with laughter,
our tongues with songs of joy.
Then it was said among the nations,
"The LORD has done great things for them." *-Psalm 126:2*

He will yet fill your mouth with laughter
and your lips with shouts of joy. *-Job 8:21*

For God's Creation

In the beginning God created the heavens and the earth. Now the earth was formless and empty, darkness was over the surface of the deep, and the Spirit of God was hovering over the waters. And God said, "Let there be light," and there was light. God saw that the light was good, and he separated the light from the darkness. God called the light "day," and the darkness he called "night." And there was evening, and there was morning—the first day. And God said, "Let there be an expanse between the waters to separate water from water." So God made the expanse and separated the water under the expanse from the water above it. And it was so. God called the expanse "sky." And there was evening, and there was morning—the second day. And God said, "Let the water under the sky be gathered to one place, and let dry ground appear." And it was so. God called the dry ground "land," and the gathered waters he called "seas." And God saw that it was good.

-Genesis 1:1-10

O LORD, our Lord, how majestic is your name in all the earth!
You have set your glory above the heavens.
From the lips of children and infants
you have ordained praise because of your enemies,
to silence the foe and the avenger.
When I consider your heavens, the work of your fingers,
the moon and the stars, which you have set in place,
what is man that you are mindful of him,
the son of man that you care for him?
You made him a little lower than the heavenly beings
and crowned him with glory and honor.
You made him ruler over the works of your hands;
you put everything under his feet:

all flocks and herds, and the beasts of the field,
the birds of the air, and the fish of the sea,
all that swim the paths of the seas.
LORD, our Lord, how majestic is your name in all the earth!   -*Psalm 8:1-9*

For the Gift of Life Itself

There is a time for everything,
and a season for every activity under heaven:
a time to be born and a time to die,
a time to plant and a time to uproot,
a time to kill and a time to heal,
a time to tear down and a time to build,
a time to weep and a time to laugh,
a time to mourn and a time to dance,
a time to scatter stones and a time to gather them,
a time to embrace and a time to refrain,
a time to search and a time to give up,
a time to keep and a time to throw away,
a time to tear and a time to mend,

a time to be silent and a time to speak,
a time to love and a time to hate,
a time for war and a time for peace.
What does the worker gain from his toil?
I have seen the burden God has laid on men.
He has made everything beautiful in its time.
He has also set eternity in the hearts of men;
yet they cannot fathom what God has done from beginning to end.

-Ecclesiastes 3:1-11

I praise you because I am fearfully and wonderfully made;
your works are wonderful, I know that full well.
My frame was not hidden from you when I was made in the secret place.
When I was woven together in the depths of the earth. *-Psalm 139:14, 15*

But our citizenship is in heaven. And we eagerly await a Savior from there, the Lord Jesus Christ, who, by the power that enables him to bring everything under his control, will transform our lowly bodies so that they will be like his glorious body.

-Philippians 3:20, 21

For Salvation

Praise be to the God and Father of our Lord Jesus Christ, who has blessed us in the heavenly realms with every spiritual blessing in Christ. For he chose us in him before the creation of the world to be holy and blameless in his sight. In love he predestined us to be adopted as his sons through Jesus Christ, in accordance with his pleasure and will— to the praise of his glorious grace, which he has freely given us in the One he loves. In him we have redemption through his blood, the forgiveness of sins, in accordance with the riches of God's grace that he lavished on us with all wisdom and understanding. And he made known to us the mystery of his will according to his good pleasure, which he purposed in Christ, to be put into effect when the times will have reached their fulfillment— to bring all things in heaven and on earth together under one head, even Christ. In him we were also chosen, having been predestined according to the plan of him who works out everything in conformity with the purpose of his will, in order that we, who were the first to hope in Christ, might be for the praise of his glory. *-Ephesians 1:3-12*

Giving thanks to the Father, who has qualified you to share
in the inheritance of the saints in the kingdom of light. *-Colossians 1:12*

For God's Love and Care

The LORD is my shepherd,
I shall not be in want.
He makes me lie down in green pastures,
he leads me beside quiet waters, he restores my soul.
He guides me in paths of righteousness for his name's sake.
Even though I walk through the valley of the shadow of death,
I will fear no evil, for you are with me;
your rod and your staff, they comfort me.
You prepare a table before me in the presence of my enemies.
You anoint my head with oil; my cup overflows.
Surely goodness and love will follow me
all the days of my life,
and I will dwell in the house of the LORD forever.   *-Psalm 23:1-6*

It is good to praise the LORD
and make music to your name, O Most High,
to proclaim your love in the morning
and your faithfulness at night,

to the music of the ten-stringed lyre
and the melody of the harp.
For you make me glad by your deeds,
O LORD; I sing for joy at the works of your hands. *-Psalm 92:1-4*

I will tell of the kindnesses of the LORD,
the deeds for which he is to be praised,
according to all the LORD has done for us—
yes, the many good things he has done for the house of Israel,
according to his compassion and many kindnesses. *-Isaiah 63:7*

And we know that in all things God works for the good of those who love him, who have been called according to his purpose. For those God foreknew he also predestined to be conformed to the likeness of his Son, that he might be the firstborn among many brothers. And those he predestined, he also called; those he called, he also justified; those he justified, he also glorified.

What, then, shall we say in response to this? If God is for us, who can be against us? He who did not spare his own Son, but gave him up for us all—how will he not also, along with him, graciously give us all things? Who will bring any charge against those whom God has chosen? It is God who justifies. Who is he that condemns? Christ Jesus, who died—more than that, who was raised to life—is at the right hand of God and is also interceding for us. Who shall separate us from the love of Christ? Shall trouble or hardship or persecution or famine or nakedness or danger or sword?

As it is written: "For your sake we face death all day long; we are considered as sheep to be slaughtered." No, in all these things we are more than conquerors through him who loved us. For I am convinced that neither death nor life, neither angels nor demons, neither the present nor the future, nor any powers, neither height nor depth, nor anything else in all creation, will be able to separate us from the love of God that is in Christ Jesus our Lord. -*Romans 8:28-39*

For God's Greatness
Sing joyfully to the LORD, you righteous;
it is fitting for the upright to praise him.
Praise the LORD with the harp;
make music to him on the ten-stringed lyre.
Sing to him a new song;
play skillfully, and shout for joy.

For the word of the LORD is right and true;
he is faithful in all he does.
The LORD loves righteousness and justice;
the earth is full of his unfailing love.   *-Psalm 33:1-5*

Come, let us sing for joy to the LORD;
let us shout aloud to the Rock of our salvation.
Let us come before him with thanksgiving
and extol him with music and song.
For the LORD is the great God,
the great King above all gods.
In his hand are the depths of the earth,
and the mountain peaks belong to him.
The sea is his, for he made it,
and his hands formed the dry land.
Come, let us bow down in worship,
let us kneel before the LORD our Maker;
for he is our God and we are the people of his pasture,
the flock under his care.   *-Psalm 95:1-7a*

Praise him with the sounding of the trumpet,
praise him with the harp and lyre,
praise him with tambourine and dancing,
praise him with the strings and flute,
praise him with the clash of cymbals,
praise him with resounding cymbals.
Let everything that has breath praise the LORD.
Praise the LORD.   -Psalm 150:3-6

Sing and Shout for Joy!

I will praise you, O LORD, with all my heart;
I will tell of all your wonders.
I will be glad and rejoice in you;
I will sing praise to your name,
O Most High.
My enemies turn back;
they stumble and perish before you.
For you have upheld my right and my cause;
you have sat on your throne,

judging righteously.
You have rebuked the nations
and destroyed the wicked;
you have blotted out their name
for ever and ever.   *-Psalm 9:1-5*

Shout with joy to God, all the earth!
Sing the glory of his name;
make his praise glorious!
Say to God, "How awesome are your deeds!
So great is your power
that your enemies cringe before you.
All the earth bows down to you;
they sing praise to you,
they sing praise to your name."   *-Psalm 66:1-4*

Delight in Children and Grandchildren, as God Does
Sons are a heritage from the LORD,
children a reward from him.   *-Psalm 127:3*

This is what the LORD says:
"I will return to Zion and dwell in Jerusalem.
Then Jerusalem will be called the City of Truth,
and the mountain of the LORD Almighty
will be called the Holy Mountain."
This is what the LORD Almighty says:
"Once again men and women of ripe old age
will sit in the streets of Jerusalem,
each with cane in hand because of his age.
The city streets will be filled
with boys and girls playing there."   *-Zechariah 8:3-5*

And Mary said: "My soul glorifies the Lord and my spirit rejoices in God my Savior,
for he has been mindful of the humble state of his servant.
From now on all generations will call me blessed,
for the Mighty One has done great things for me—holy is his name.
His mercy extends to those who fear him,
from generation to generation.
He has performed mighty deeds with his arm;

he has scattered those who are proud in their inmost thoughts.
He has brought down rulers from their thrones
but has lifted up the humble.
He has filled the hungry with good things
but has sent the rich away empty.
He has helped his servant Israel,
remembering to be merciful
to Abraham and his descendants forever,
even as he said to our fathers."
Mary stayed with Elizabeth for about three months and then returned home.

-Luke 1:46-56

> And Jesus grew in wisdom and stature, and in favor with God and men.
> *-Luke 2:52*

After six days Jesus took with him Peter, James and John the brother of James, and led them up a high mountain by themselves. There he was transfigured before them. His face shone like the sun, and his clothes became as white as the light. Just then there appeared before them Moses and Elijah, talking with Jesus.

Peter said to Jesus, "Lord, it is good for us to be here. If you wish, I will put up three shelters—one for you, one for Moses and one for Elijah."

While he was still speaking, a bright cloud enveloped them, and a voice from the cloud said, "This is my Son, whom I love; with him I am well pleased. Listen to him!"

-Matthew 17:1-5

Whoever humbles himself like this child is the greatest in the kingdom of heaven.

-Matthew 18:4

Become More Childlike Yourself!

They send forth their children as a flock; their little ones dance about.

-Job 21:11

Let them praise his name with dancing and make music to him
with tambourine and harp.

-Psalm 149:3

But I am only a little child and do not know how to carry out my duties.

-1 Kings 3:7b

26

He tends his flock like a shepherd:
He gathers the lambs in his arms
and carries them close to his heart;
he gently leads those that have young.
-Isaiah 40:11

"Ah, Sovereign LORD," I said, "I do not know how to speak; I am only a child."

But the LORD said to me, "Do not say, 'I am only a child.' You must go to everyone I send you to and say whatever I command you. Do not be afraid of them, for I am with you and will rescue you," declares the LORD. *-Jeremiah 1:6-8*

In regard to evil be infants, but in your thinking be adults.
-I Corinthians 14:20b

With your help I can advance against a troop;
with my God I can scale a wall. *-II Samuel 22:30*

When you walk, your steps will not be hampered;
when you run, you will not stumble.
-Proverbs 4:12

But for you who revere my name,
the sun of righteousness
will rise with healing in its wings.
And you will go out
and leap like calves released from the stall.
-Malachi 4:2

Therefore, since we are surrounded by such a great cloud of witnesses,
let us throw off everything that hinders and the sin that so easily entangles,
and let us run with perseverance the race marked out for us.
-Hebrews 12:1

FOR PERSONAL PRAYER:
Heavenly Father, help me to view my advancing age as a blessing rather than a liability. I know this goes against everything the world is telling me, because "staying young" is supposed to be the goal. But I want to listen more closely to what You are telling me, starting with this one day. Amen.

♦ Chapter 2 ♦

What kinds of wisdom can I offer the younger generations?

I may not be the smartest person alive," said Howard. "But I know I've learned a lot during my years of living so far. I've got some things to say to young people if they're willing to hear them.

"Experience is a great teacher. It would be great to be able to help my grandchildren avoid some of the mistakes I've made. I think I could do that by just letting them hear more about my life story, about the kinds of decisions I've made over the years. Some of those things turned out okay and other things didn't. But I can point to the faithfulness of my Lord through everything that's happened."

FOR MEMORY:

Even when I am old and gray, do not forsake me, O God,
till I declare your power to the next generation,
your might to all who are to come. *-Psalm 71:18*

FOR SILENT REFLECTION:

♦ *In what ways did my own parents and grandparents help prepare me for life? Or: What do I wish they would have taught me about how to live before I had to learn those things "the hard way"?*

♦ *What special knowledge or wisdom have I picked up over the years?*

♦ *How could I begin to bequeath that wisdom to my grandchildren? What methods might work the best?*

You Do Have Wisdom to Bequeath

Does not wisdom call out?
Does not understanding raise her voice?
On the heights along the way, where the paths meet,

she takes her stand;
beside the gates leading into the city,
at the entrances, she cries aloud:
"To you, O men, I call out;
I raise my voice to all mankind.
You who are simple, gain prudence;
you who are foolish, gain understanding.
Listen, for I have worthy things to say;
I open my lips to speak what is right.
My mouth speaks what is true,
for my lips detest wickedness.
All the words of my mouth are just;
none of them is crooked or perverse.
To the discerning all of them are right;
they are faultless to those who have knowledge.
Choose my instruction instead of silver,
knowledge rather than choice gold,
for wisdom is more precious than rubies,
and nothing you desire can compare with her. *-Proverbs 8:1-11*

Remind Your Grandchildren Not to Forget Their Creator

Remember your Creator in the days of your youth,
before the days of trouble come
and the years approach when you will say,
"I find no pleasure in them"—
before the sun and the light and the moon and the stars grow dark,
and the clouds return after the rain;
when the keepers of the house tremble, and the strong men stoop,
when the grinders cease because they are few,
and those looking through the windows grow dim;
when the doors to the street are closed and the sound of grinding fades;
when men rise up at the sound of birds, but all their songs grow faint;
when men are afraid of heights and of dangers in the streets;
when the almond tree blossoms
and the grasshopper drags himself along and desire no longer is stirred.
Then man goes to his eternal home and mourners go about the streets.
Remember him—before the silver cord is severed, or the golden bowl is broken;
before the pitcher is shattered at the spring, or the wheel broken at the well,

and the dust returns to the ground it came from,
and the spirit returns to God who gave it. . . .
For God will bring every deed into judgment,
including every hidden thing, whether it is good or evil. *-Ecclesiastes 12:1-7, 14*

♦ Biblical Values to Teach Your Grandchildren ♦

Compassion

As a father has compassion on his children,
so the LORD has compassion on those who fear him. *-Psalm 103:13*

I will plant her for myself in the land;
I will show my love to the one I called "Not my loved one."
I will say to those called "Not my people," "You are my people";
and they will say, "You are my God." *-Hosea 2:23*

Be merciful to those who doubt; snatch others from the fire and save them; to others
show mercy, mixed with fear—hating even the clothing stained by corrupted flesh.
-Jude 22, 23

Faith

Even though I walk
through the valley of the shadow of death,
I will fear no evil, for you are with me;
your rod and your staff, they comfort me. *-Psalm 23:4*

Say to those with fearful hearts,
"Be strong, do not fear; your God will come,
he will come with vengeance;
with divine retribution he will come to save you." *-Isaiah 35:4*

I tell you the truth, if you have faith as small as a mustard seed, you can say to this
mountain, 'Move from here to there' and it will move.
Nothing will be impossible for you. *-Matthew 17:20b*

For nothing is impossible with God. *-Luke 1:37*

Without faith it is impossible to please God, because anyone who comes to him must
believe that he exists and that he rewards those who earnestly seek him.
-Hebrews 11:6

Wisdom

To the man who pleases him,
God gives wisdom, knowledge and happiness,
but to the sinner he gives the task of gathering and storing up wealth
to hand it over to the one who pleases God.
-Ecclesastes 2:26a

For God, who said, "Let light shine out of darkness," made his light shine in our hearts
to give us the light of the knowledge of the glory of God in the face of Christ.
-II Corinthians 4:6

If any of you lacks wisdom, he should ask God, who gives generously to all without
finding fault, and it will be given to him.
-James 1:5

We know also that the Son of God has come and has given us understanding, so that we
may know him who is true. And we are in him who is true—even in his Son Jesus
Christ. He is the true God and eternal life.
-I John 5:20

Obedience to God

If they obey and serve him, they will spend the rest of their days in prosperity
and their years in contentment.
-*Job 36:11*

May the words of my mouth
and the meditation of my heart be pleasing in your sight,
O LORD, my Rock and my Redeemer. -*Psalm 19:14*

No one can serve two masters. Either he will hate the one and love the other, or he
will be devoted to the one and despise the other.
You cannot serve both God and Money.
-*Matthew 6:24*

We know that we have come to know him if we obey his commands.
-*1 John 2:3*

So whether you eat or drink or whatever you do, do it all for the glory of God.
-*1 Corinthians 10:31*

Forgiveness

For if you forgive men when they sin against you,
your heavenly Father will also forgive you. *-Matthew 6:14*

And when you stand praying, if you hold anything against anyone, forgive him,
so that your Father in heaven may forgive you your sins. *-Mark 11:25*

If your enemy is hungry, feed him; if he is thirsty, give him something to drink.
In doing this, you will heap burning coals on his head. *-Romans 12:20*

Honesty

Keep me from deceitful ways;
be gracious to me through your law.
I have chosen the way of truth;
I have set my heart on your laws.
I hold fast to your statutes, O LORD;
do not let me be put to shame.
I run in the path of your commands,
for you have set my heart free.

Teach me, O LORD, to follow your decrees;
then I will keep them to the end. *-Psalm 119:29-33*

Do not lie to each other, since you have taken off your old self
with its practices and have put on the new self,
which is being renewed in knowledge in the image of its Creator. *-Colossians 3:9, 10*

Humility

Better to be lowly in spirit and among the oppressed
than to share plunder with the proud. *-Proverbs 16:19*

Therefore, whoever humbles himself like this child
is the greatest in the kingdom of heaven. *-Matthew 18:4*

But he gives us more grace. That is why Scripture says:
"God opposes the proud but gives grace to the humble." *-James 4:6*

Humble yourselves, therefore, under God's mighty hand,
that he may lift you up in due time. *-1 Peter 5:6*

Peacefulness

The fruit of righteousness will be peace;
the effect of righteousness will be quietness and confidence forever. *-Isaiah 32:17*

Peace I leave with you; my peace I give you. I do not give to you as the world gives.
Do not let your hearts be troubled and do not be afraid. *-John 14:27*

Let the peace of Christ rule in your hearts,
since as members of one body you were called to peace. And be thankful.
-Colossians 3:15

Now may the Lord of peace himself give you peace at all times and in every way.
The Lord be with all of you. *-II Thessalonians 3:16*

Thoughtfulness

In everything, do to others what you would have them do to you,
for this sums up the Law and the Prophets. *-Matthew 7:12*

I tell you the truth, whatever you did for one of the least of these brothers of mine,
you did for me. *-Matthew 25:40b*

Love your enemies, do good to those who hate you. -*Luke 6:27b*

And now these three remain: faith, hope and love.
But the greatest of these is love.
-*1 Corinthians 13:13*

Happiness
The LORD has done great things for us,
and we are filled with joy. -*Psalm 126:3*

A happy heart makes the face cheerful, but heartache crushes the spirit.
-*Proverbs 15:13*

A cheerful heart is good medicine, but a crushed spirit dries up the bones.
-*Proverbs 17:22*

I know that there is nothing better for men
than to be happy and do good while they live.
-*Ecclesiastes 3:12*

♦ Teach Your Grandchildren, by Word and Example . . . ♦

To Avoid Bad Advice and Bad Company

My son, if sinners entice you, do not give in to them.
If they say, "Come along with us;
let's lie in wait for someone's blood, let's waylay some harmless soul;
let's swallow them alive, like the grave,
and whole, like those who go down to the pit;
we will get all sorts of valuable things and fill our houses with plunder;
throw in your lot with us, and we will share a common purse"—
my son, do not go along with them,
do not set foot on their paths; for their feet rush into sin,
they are swift to shed blood.
How useless to spread a net in full view of all the birds!
These men lie in wait for their own blood;
they waylay only themselves!
Such is the end of all who go after ill-gotten gain;
it takes away the lives of those who get it.

-*Proverbs 1:10-19*

To Accept Correction and Discipline for Its Benefits

Discipline your son, and he will give you peace;
he will bring delight to your soul. *-Proverbs 29:17*

My son, do not despise the LORD'S discipline
and do not resent his rebuke,
because the LORD disciplines those he loves,
as a father the son he delights in. *-Proverbs 3:11, 12*

Wisdom is found on the lips of the discerning,
but a rod is for the back of him who lacks judgment. *-Proverbs 10:13*

He who spares the rod hates his son,
but he who loves him is careful to discipline him. *-Proverbs 13:24*

Discipline your son, for in that there is hope;
do not be a willing party to his death. *-Proverbs 19:18*

Blows and wounds cleanse away evil,
and beatings purge the inmost being. *-Proverbs 20:30*

Folly is bound up in the heart of a child,
but the rod of discipline will drive it far from him. *-Proverbs 22:15*

Do not withhold discipline from a child;
if you punish him with the rod, he will not die.
Punish him with the rod and save his soul from death. *-Proverbs 23:13, 14*

The rod of correction imparts wisdom,
but a child left to himself disgraces his mother. *-Proverbs 29:15*

To Appreciate Parental Guidance
Listen, my sons, to a father's instruction;
pay attention and gain understanding.
I give you sound learning,
so do not forsake my teaching.
When I was a boy in my father's house,
still tender, and an only child of my mother,
he taught me and said, "Lay hold of my words
with all your heart; keep my commands and you will live.

Get wisdom, get understanding;
do not forget my words or swerve from them.
Do not forsake wisdom, and she will protect you;
love her, and she will watch over you.
Wisdom is supreme; therefore get wisdom.
Though it cost all you have, get understanding.
Esteem her, and she will exalt you; embrace her, and she will honor you.
She will set a garland of grace on your head and present you with a crown of splendor."
-Proverbs 4:1-9

To Handle Money Wisely

Do not wear yourself out to get rich;
have the wisdom to show restraint.
Cast but a glance at riches, and they are gone,
for they will surely sprout wings and fly off to the sky like an eagle.
-Proverbs 23:4, 5

A good name is more desirable than great riches;
to be esteemed is better than silver or gold. *-Proverbs 22:1*

One man pretends to be rich, yet has nothing;
another pretends to be poor, yet has great wealth.
A man's riches may ransom his life, but a poor man hears no threat.
-Proverbs 13:7, 8

To Recognize the Value of Hard Work
I went past the field of the sluggard,
past the vineyard of the man who lacks judgment;
thorns had come up everywhere,
the ground was covered with weeds,
and the stone wall was in ruins.
I applied my heart to what I observed and learned a lesson from what I saw:
A little sleep, a little slumber,
a little folding of the hands to rest—
and poverty will come on you like a bandit
and scarcity like an armed man. *-Proverbs 24:30-34*

The sluggard says, "There is a lion in the road,
a fierce lion roaming the streets!"

As a door turns on its hinges,
so a sluggard turns on his bed.
The sluggard buries his hand in the dish;
he is too lazy to bring it back to his mouth.
The sluggard is wiser in his own eyes
than seven men who answer discreetly.
-Proverbs 26:13-16

Be sure you know the condition of your flocks,
give careful attention to your herds;
for riches do not endure forever,
and a crown is not secure for all generations.
When the hay is removed and new growth appears
and the grass from the hills is gathered in,
the lambs will provide you with clothing,
and the goats with the price of a field.
You will have plenty of goats' milk to feed you
and your family and to nourish your servant girls.
-Proverbs 27:23-27

FOR PERSONAL PRAYER:

Lord, You have taught me valuable lessons over the years. Help me to find ways to communicate Your wisdom, grace, and love to my grandchildren. Give them ears to hear and to learn. And give me the courage to share about both my failures and successes, for their benefit. Amen.

♦ Chapter 3 ♦

'How can I keep my spiritual life going strong?'

I feel as though I'm more free to follow God's leading in my life than ever before," said MaryEllen. "I used to be so busy, but life has slowed down a bit. But I don't see that as a disadvantage. Actually, it's a blessing to be able to focus more energy on my spiritual life. I'm finding new ways of learning about God and studying the Scriptures. My grandchildren even suggested that I get a computer to help me in my Bible study!"

"There are so many opportunities for fellowship and church involvement, too. And I do find myself having more time for prayer. I'm praying that God will become more and more real to me every day."

FOR MEMORY:
Gray hair is a crown of splendor;
it is attained by a righteous life.
-Proverbs 16:31

FOR SILENT REFLECTION:

◆ *What new opportunities for fellowship and spiritual growth seem to be coming my way?*

◆ *How is my prayer life going? In what ways am I now more available for a ministry of prayer in my church?*

◆ *What is God trying to tell me in the periods of silence that enter my days? What have I learned about Him lately?*

◆ *What part can I play in encouraging the spiritual growth of my children and grandchildren? What practical steps could I take toward that end?*

You Need Supernatural Help to Be a Good Grandparent!

Every good and perfect gift is from above, coming down from the Father of the heavenly lights, who does not change like shifting shadows. *-James 1:17*

The God who made the world and everything in it is the Lord of heaven and earth and does not live in temples built by hands. And he is not served by human hands, as if he needed anything, because he himself gives all men life and breath and everything else. From one man he made every nation of men, that they should inhabit the whole earth; and he determined the times set for them and the exact places where they should live. God did this so that men would seek him and perhaps reach out for him and find him, though he is not far from each one of us. 'For in him we live and move and have our being.' *-Acts 17:24-28a*

♦ Get to Know Your Helper . . . ♦
I Am the Bread of Life

Then Jesus declared, "I am the bread of life. He who comes to me will never go hungry, and he who believes in me will never be thirsty. But as I told you, you have seen me and still you do not believe. All that the Father gives me will come to me, and whoever comes to me I will never drive away. For I have come down from heaven not to do my will but to do the will of him who sent me. And this is the will of him who sent me, that I shall lose none of all that he has given me, but raise them up at the last day. For my Father's will is that everyone who looks to the Son and believes in him shall have eternal life, and I will raise him up at the last day." *-John 6:35-40*

I Am the Light of the World

When Jesus spoke again to the people, he said, "I am the light of the world. Whoever follows me will never walk in darkness, but will have the light of life." *-John 8:12*

As long as it is day, we must do the work of him who sent me. Night is coming, when no one can work. While I am in the world, I am the light of the world. *-John 9:4, 5*

I Am the Gate of Salvation

Therefore Jesus said again, "I tell you the truth, I am the gate for the sheep. All who ever came before me were thieves and robbers, but the sheep did not listen to them. I am the gate; whoever enters through me will be saved. He will come in and go out, and find pasture. The thief comes only to steal and kill and destroy; I have come that they may have life, and have it to the full." *-John 10:7-10*

I Am the Good Shepherd

I am the good shepherd. The good shepherd lays down his life for the sheep. The hired hand is not the shepherd who owns the sheep. So when he sees the wolf coming, he abandons the sheep and runs away. Then the wolf attacks the flock and scatters it. The man runs away because he is a hired hand and cares nothing for the sheep. I am the good shepherd; I know my sheep and my sheep know me— just as the Father knows me and I know the Father—and I lay down my life for the sheep. I have other sheep that are not of this sheep pen. I must bring them also. They too will listen to my voice, and there shall be one flock and one shepherd. The reason my Father loves me is that I lay down my life—only to take it up again. No one takes it from me, but I lay it down of my own accord. I have authority to lay it down and authority to take it up again. This command I received from my Father. *-John 10:11-18*

I Am the Resurrection and the Life

"Lord," Martha said to Jesus, "if you had been here, my brother would not have died. But I know that even now God will give you whatever you ask." Jesus said to her, "Your brother will rise again." Martha answered, "I know he will rise again in the resurrection at the last day." Jesus said to her, "I am the resurrection and the life. He who believes in me will live, even though he dies; and whoever lives and believes in me will never die. Do you believe this?" *-John 11:21-26*

I Am the Way, the Truth, the Life

Jesus answered, "I am the way and the truth and the life.
No one comes to the Father except through me." *-John 14:6*

I Am the True Vine

I am the true vine, and my Father is the gardener. He cuts off every branch in me that bears no fruit, while every branch that does bear fruit he prunes so that it will be even more fruitful. You are already clean because of the word I have spoken to you. Remain in me, and I will remain in you. No branch can bear fruit by itself; it must remain in the vine. Neither can you bear fruit unless you remain in me. I am the vine; you are the branches. If a man remains in me and I in him, he will bear much fruit; apart from me you can do nothing. If anyone does not remain in me, he is like a branch that is thrown away and withers; such branches are picked up, thrown into the fire and burned.

If you remain in me and my words remain in you, ask whatever you wish,
and it will be given you. *-John 15:1-7*

◆ Jesus Is . . . ◆

Your Shepherd

He will stand and shepherd his flock in the strength of the LORD,
in the majesty of the name of the LORD his God.
And they will live securely, for then his greatness will reach to the ends of the earth.
And he will be their peace. *-Micah 5:4*

And when the Chief Shepherd appears, you will receive the crown of glory
that will never fade away. *-I Peter 5:4*

Your Example
You call me 'Teacher' and 'Lord,' and rightly so, for that is what I am.
-John 13:13

A new command I give you: Love one another.
As I have loved you, so you must love one another.
-John 13:34

Each of us should please his neighbor for his good, to build him up. *-Romans 15:2*

Live a life of love, just as Christ loved us
and gave himself up for us as a fragrant offering and sacrifice to God.
-Ephesians 5:2

Your attitude should be the same as that of Christ Jesus: Who, being in very nature
God, did not consider equality with God something to be grasped, but made himself

nothing, taking the very nature of a servant, being made in human likeness.
And being found in appearance as a man, he humbled himself
and became obedient to death—even death on a cross! *-Philippians 2:5-8*

Your Prayer Partner: He Prays for You

I pray for them. I am not praying for the world, but for those you have given me, for they are yours. All I have is yours, and all you have is mine. And glory has come to me through them. I will remain in the world no longer, but they are still in the world, and I am coming to you. Holy Father, protect them by the power of your name—the name you gave me—so that they may be one as we are one. While I was with them, I protected them and kept them safe by that name you gave me. None has been lost except the one doomed to destruction so that Scripture would be fulfilled. "I am coming to you now, but I say these things while I am still in the world, so that they may have the full measure of my joy within them. I have given them your word and the world has hated them, for they are not of the world any more than I am of the world. My prayer is not that you take them out of the world but that you protect them from the evil one.

-John 17:9-15

55

Your Fellow Struggler against Temptation

The tempter came to him and said, "If you are the Son of God, tell these stones to become bread." Jesus answered, "It is written: 'Man does not live on bread alone, but on every word that comes from the mouth of God.'" Then the devil took him to the holy city and had him stand on the highest point of the temple. "If you are the Son of God," he said, "throw yourself down. For it is written: 'He will command his angels concerning you, and they will lift you up in their hands, so that you will not strike your foot against a stone.'" Jesus answered him, "It is also written: 'Do not put the Lord your God to the test.'" Again, the devil took him to a very high mountain and showed him all the kingdoms of the world and their splendor. All this I will give you," he said, "if you will bow down and worship me." Jesus said to him, "Away from me, Satan! For it is written: 'Worship the Lord your God, and serve him only.'" Then the devil left him, and angels came and attended him. *-Matthew 4:3-11*

Because he himself suffered when he was tempted,
he is able to help those who are being tempted. *-Hebrews 2:18*

For we do not have a high priest who is unable to sympathize with our weaknesses, but we have one who has been tempted in every way, just as we are—yet was without sin.
-Hebrews 4:15

Jesus Is God: He Claimed to Be Deity

In the beginning was the Word, and the Word was with God, and the Word was God. . . . The Word became flesh and made his dwelling among us. We have seen his glory, the glory of the One and Only, who came from the Father, full of grace and truth. *-John 1:1, 14*

Coming to his hometown, he began teaching the people in their synagogue, and they were amazed. "Where did this man get this wisdom and these miraculous powers?" they asked. *-Matthew 13:54*

Then Jesus came to them and said, "All authority in heaven and on earth has been given to me." *-Matthew 28:18*

But Jesus remained silent. The high priest said to him, "I charge you under oath by the living God: Tell us if you are the Christ, the Son of God." "Yes, it is as you say," Jesus replied. "But I say to all of you: In the future you will see the Son of Man sitting at the right hand of the Mighty One and coming on the clouds of heaven." Then the high priest tore his clothes and said, "He has spoken blasphemy! Why do we need any more witnesses? Look, now you have heard the blasphemy." *-Matthew 26:63-65*

He said to them, "How foolish you are, and how slow of heart to believe all that the prophets have spoken! Did not the Christ have to suffer these things and then enter his glory?" And beginning with Moses and all the Prophets, he explained to them what was said in all the Scriptures concerning himself. *-Luke 24:25-27*

The woman said, "I know that Messiah" (called Christ) "is coming. When he comes, he will explain everything to us." Then Jesus declared, "I who speak to you am he."

-John 4:25, 26

The Jews gathered around him, saying, "How long will you keep us in suspense? If you are the Christ, tell us plainly." Jesus answered, "I did tell you, but you do not believe. The miracles I do in my Father's name speak for me, but you do not believe because you are not my sheep. My sheep listen to my voice; I know them, and they follow me. I give them eternal life, and they shall never perish; no one can snatch them out of my hand. My Father, who has given them to me, is greater than all; no one can snatch them out of my Father's hand. I and the Father are one." *-John 10:24-30*

♦ You Have More Time for Exploring Who God Is ♦
He Is All-Powerful

The LORD is slow to anger and great in power;
the LORD will not leave the guilty unpunished.
His way is in the whirlwind and the storm,
and clouds are the dust of his feet.
He rebukes the sea and dries it up;
he makes all the rivers run dry.
Bashan and Carmel wither and the blossoms of Lebanon fade.
The mountains quake before him and the hills melt away.
The earth trembles at his presence, the world and all who live in it.
Who can withstand his indignation?
Who can endure his fierce anger?
His wrath is poured out like fire; the rocks are shattered before him. *-Nahum 1:3-6*

What, then, shall we say in response to this? If God is for us, who can be against us?
-Romans 8:31

He Is All-Knowing and Wise

The LORD brought me, [Wisdom],
forth as the first of his works, before his deeds of old;
I was appointed from eternity, from the beginning, before the world began.
When there were no oceans, I was given birth,
when there were no springs abounding with water;
before the mountains were settled in place,
before the hills, I was given birth,
before he made the earth or its fields or any of the dust of the world.
I was there when he set the heavens in place,
when he marked out the horizon on the face of the deep,
when he established the clouds above and fixed securely the fountains of the deep,
when he gave the sea its boundary so the waters would not overstep his command,
and when he marked out the foundations of the earth.
Then I was the craftsman at his side.
I was filled with delight day after day,
rejoicing always in his presence,
rejoicing in his whole world and delighting in mankind.

-Proverbs 8:22-31

And even the very hairs of your head are all numbered.
-Matthew 10:30

He Is Long-Suffering

Rend your heart and not your garments.
Return to the LORD your God,
for he is gracious and compassionate,
slow to anger and abounding in love,
and he relents from sending calamity. *-Joel 2:13*

How long, O LORD, must I call for help, but you do not listen?
Or cry out to you, "Violence!" but you do not save?
Why do you make me look at injustice?
Why do you tolerate wrong?
Destruction and violence are before me;
there is strife, and conflict abounds.
Therefore the law is paralyzed,
and justice never prevails.

The wicked hem in the righteous,
so that justice is perverted. *-Habakkuk 1:2-4*

Or do you show contempt for the riches of his kindness, tolerance and patience, not
realizing that God's kindness leads you toward repentance?
-Romans 2:4
May the God who gives endurance and encouragement
give you a spirit of unity among yourselves
as you follow Christ Jesus. *-Romans 15:5*

He Is Merciful

You are a forgiving God, gracious and compassionate,
slow to anger and abounding in love. *-Nehemiah 9:17b*

For this is what the high and lofty One says—
he who lives forever, whose name is holy:
"I live in a high and holy place,
but also with him who is contrite and lowly in spirit,
to revive the spirit of the lowly and to revive the heart of the contrite.

I will not accuse forever, nor will I always be angry,
for then the spirit of man would grow faint before me—
the breath of man that I have created.
I was enraged by his sinful greed;
I punished him, and hid my face in anger,
yet he kept on in his willful ways.
I have seen his ways, but I will heal him;
I will guide him and restore comfort to him,
creating praise on the lips of the mourners in Israel.
Peace, peace, to those far and near," says the LORD.
"And I will heal them." *-Isaiah 57:15-19*

Be merciful, just as your Father is merciful. *-Luke 6:36*

For there is no difference between Jew and Gentile—
the same Lord is Lord of all and richly blesses all who call on him. *-Romans 10:12*

He Is Faithful

God is not unjust; he will not forget your work and the love you have shown him as you have helped his people and continue to help them. . . . When God made his promise to Abraham, since there was no one greater for him to swear by, he swore by himself, saying, "I will surely bless you and give you many descendants." And so after waiting patiently, Abraham received what was promised. Men swear by someone greater than themselves, and the oath confirms what is said and puts an end to all argument. Because God wanted to make the unchanging nature of his purpose very clear to the heirs of what was promised, he confirmed it with an oath. God did this so that, by two unchangeable things in which it is impossible for God to lie, we who have fled to take hold of the hope offered to us may be greatly encouraged. We have this hope as an anchor for the soul, firm and secure. It enters the inner sanctuary behind the curtain. -*Hebrews 6:10, 13-19*

So then, those who suffer according to God's will should commit themselves to their faithful Creator and continue to do good. -*I Peter 4:19*

FOR PERSONAL PRAYER:

Lord God, may I be open today to Your still, small voice. Lead me into a brand new exploration of my spiritual gifts, and show me the opportunities for using those gifts in Your service. Keep my spiritual growth the focus of my grandparenting years. Amen.

♦ Chapter 4 ♦

'What things can I do to help my grandchildren feel blessed?'

I'm thinking more and more about what it means to a child to feel secure and loved," commented Esther. "So much has to do with how the family members interact with one another, and how much love and acceptance comes from the parents and extended family.

"I want to be a part of the structure from which that kind of blessing flows to my grandchildren. The whole idea is biblical, too. I've found many scriptural examples of parents and grandparents blessing their children. But it was more than just handing out little compliments. It was a serious announcement of their place in history and in God's plans. That's what I want for my children and my children's children."

> ### FOR MEMORY:
> Come, my children, listen to me;
> I will teach you the fear of the LORD.
> -Psalm 34:11

FOR SILENT REFLECTION:

♦ *To what extent did I feel secure and loved in my family of origin?*

♦ *What things did my parents and grandparents do that helped me feel (or not feel) blessed in that way?*

♦ *What could I do with my children or grandchildren that would help them know more of my personal blessing upon them? more of God's blessing?*

♦ *How willing am I to admit any past parenting mistakes? What would it take for me to start afresh, seeking to heal any broken relationships with my children?*

All Children Crave Parental Blessings!

After Isaac finished blessing him and Jacob had scarcely left his father's presence, his brother Esau came in from hunting. He too prepared some tasty food and brought it to his father. Then he said to him, "My father, sit up and eat some of my game, so that you may give me your blessing." His father Isaac asked him, "Who are you?" "I am your son," he answered, "your firstborn, Esau." Isaac trembled violently and said, "Who was it, then, that hunted game and brought it to me? I ate it just before you came and I blessed him— and indeed he will be blessed!" When Esau heard his father's words, he burst out with a loud and bitter cry and said to his father, "Bless me—me too, my father!". . . Esau said to his father, "Do you have only one blessing, my father? Bless me too, my father!" Then Esau wept aloud. -*Genesis 27:30-34,38*

My God, my God,
why have you forsaken me?
Why are you so far from saving me,
so far from the words of my groaning? -*Psalm 22:1*

Will the Lord reject forever?
Will he never show his favor again?
Has his unfailing love vanished forever?
Has his promise failed for all time?
Has God forgotten to be merciful?
Has he in anger withheld his compassion? -*Psalm 77:7-9*

Why do you say, O Jacob, and complain, O Israel,
"My way is hidden from the LORD;
my cause is disregarded by my God"?
Do you not know? Have you not heard?
The LORD is the everlasting God,
the Creator of the ends of the earth.
He will not grow tired or weary,
and his understanding no one can fathom. *-Isaiah 40:27, 28*

Jacob Blessed His Grandchildren

When Israel saw the sons of Joseph, he asked, "Who are these?" "They are the sons God has given me here," Joseph said to his father. Then Israel said, "Bring them to me so I may bless them."

Now Israel's eyes were failing because of old age, and he could hardly see. So Joseph brought his sons close to him, and his father kissed them and embraced them. Israel said to Joseph, "I never expected to see your face again, and now God has allowed me to see your children too."

Then Joseph removed them from Israel's knees and bowed down with his face to the ground. And Joseph took both of them, Ephraim on his right toward Israel's left hand and Manasseh on his left toward Israel's right hand, and brought them close to him. But Israel reached out his right hand and put it on Ephraim's head, though he was the younger, and crossing his arms, he put his left hand on Manasseh's head, even though Manasseh was the firstborn.

Then he blessed Joseph and said, "May the God before whom my fathers Abraham and Isaac walked, the God who has been my shepherd all my life to this day, the Angel who has delivered me from all harm—may he bless these boys. May they be called by my name and the names of my fathers Abraham and Isaac, and may they increase greatly upon the earth."

When Joseph saw his father placing his right hand on Ephraim's head he was displeased; so he took hold of his father's hand to move it from Ephraim's head to Manasseh's head. Joseph said to him, "No, my father, this one is the firstborn; put your right hand on his head."

But his father refused and said, "I know, my son, I know. He too will become a people, and he too will become great. Nevertheless, his younger brother will be greater than he, and his descendants will become a group of nations."

He blessed them that day and said, "In your name will Israel pronounce this blessing: 'May God make you like Ephraim and Manasseh.'" *-Genesis 48:8-20a*

Bless Your Grandchildren Too:

Blessed are you (_____*Your Grandchild's Name*_____),
when you do not walk in the counsel of the wicked
or stand in the way of sinners or sit in the seat of mockers.
But your delight is in the law of the LORD,
and on his law may you meditate day and night.
Then you will be like a tree planted by streams of water,
which yields its fruit in season
and whose leaf does not wither.
Whatever you do will prosper.
Not so the wicked!
They are like chaff that the wind blows away.
Therefore the wicked will not stand in the judgment,
nor sinners in the assembly of the righteous.
For the LORD watches over the way of the righteous,
but the way of the wicked will perish.
-Psalm 1:1-6

My grandson/granddaughter, (_____*Name*_____),
if you accept my words
and store up my commands within you,
turning your ear to wisdom
and applying your heart to understanding,
and if you call out for insight
and cry aloud for understanding,
and if you look for it as for silver
and search for it as for hidden treasure,
then you will understand the fear of the LORD
and find the knowledge of God.
For the LORD gives wisdom,
and from his mouth come knowledge and understanding.
He holds victory in store for the upright,
he is a shield to those whose walk is blameless,
for he guards the course of the just
and protects the way of his faithful ones.
-*Proverbs 2:1-8*

Trust in the LORD with all your heart, (_____*Name*_____),
and lean not on your own understanding;
in all your ways acknowledge him,
and he will make your paths straight. -*Proverbs 3:5, 6*

I pray that out of his glorious riches [God] may strengthen you, (_____*Name*_____), with power through his Spirit in your inner being, so that Christ may dwell in your hearts through faith. And I pray that you, being rooted and established in love, may have power, together with all the saints, to grasp how wide and long and high and deep is the love of Christ, and to know this love that surpasses knowledge—that you may be filled to the measure of all the fullness of God. -*Ephesians 3:16-19*

Tell Your Grandchildren of God's Blessings

If you then, though you are evil, know how to give good gifts to your children, how much more will your Father in heaven give the Holy Spirit to those who ask him!"

-*Luke 11:13*

On the last and greatest day of the Feast, Jesus stood and said in a loud voice, "If anyone is thirsty, let him come to me and drink. Whoever believes in me, as the Scripture has said, streams of living water will flow from within him." By this he meant the Spirit, whom those who believed in him were later to receive. Up to that time the Spirit had not been given, since Jesus had not yet been glorified. *-John 7:37-39*

And I will ask the Father, and he will give you another Counselor to be with you forever—the Spirit of truth. The world cannot accept him, because it neither sees him nor knows him. But you know him, for he lives with you and will be in you. . . . But the Counselor, the Holy Spirit, whom the Father will send in my name, will teach you all things and will remind you of everything I have said to you. Peace I leave with you; my peace I give you. I do not give to you as the world gives. Do not let your hearts be troubled and do not be afraid. *-John 14:16, 17, 26, 27*

Now I commit you to God and to the word of his grace, which can build you up and give you an inheritance among all those who are sanctified. *-Acts 20:32*

To him who is able to keep you from falling and to present you before his glorious presence without fault and with great joy—to the only God our Savior be glory, majesty, power and authority, through Jesus Christ our Lord, before all ages, now and forevermore! Amen. *-Jude 24, 25*

Help Your Grandchildren Acknowledge Their Creaturehood

So God created man in his own image, in the image of God he created him; male and female he created them. God blessed them and said to them, "Be fruitful and increase in number; fill the earth and subdue it. Rule over the fish of the sea and the birds of the air and over every living creature that moves on the ground." Then God said, "I give you every seed-bearing plant on the face of the whole earth and every tree that has fruit with seed in it. They will be yours for food. And to all the beasts of the earth and all the birds of the air and all the creatures that move on the ground—everything that has the breath of life in it—I give every green plant for food." And it was so.

God saw all that he had made, and it was very good. *-Genesis 1:27-31a*

> I praise you because I am fearfully and wonderfully made;
> your works are wonderful, I know that full well.
> My frame was not hidden from you
> when I was made in the secret place.
> When I was woven together in the depths of the earth,
> your eyes saw my unformed body.
> All the days ordained for me were written in your book
> before one of them came to be. *-Psalm 139:14-16*

O LORD, our Lord, how majestic is your name in all the earth!
You have set your glory above the heavens.
– From the lips of children and infants you have ordained praise
because of your enemies, to silence the foe and the avenger.
When I consider your heavens, the work of your fingers,
the moon and the stars, which you have set in place,
what is man that you are mindful of him,
the son of man that you care for him?
You made him a little lower than the heavenly beings
and crowned him with glory and honor.
You made him ruler over the works of your hands; you put everything under his feet:
all flocks and herds, and the beasts of the field,
the birds of the air, and the fish of the sea,
all that swim the paths of the seas.
O LORD, our Lord, how majestic is your name in all the earth! *-Psalm 8:1-9*

Lead Your Grandchildren to Personal Salvation

At that time the disciples came to Jesus and asked, "Who is the greatest in the kingdom of heaven?" He called a little child and had him stand among them. And he said: "I tell you the truth, unless you change and become like little children, you will never enter the kingdom of heaven. Therefore, whoever humbles himself like this child is the greatest in the kingdom of heaven. And whoever welcomes a little child like this in my name welcomes me. But if anyone causes one of these little ones who believe in me to sin, it would be better for him to have a large millstone hung around his neck and to be drowned in the depths of the sea. Woe to the world because of the things that cause people to sin! Such things must come, but woe to the man through whom they come! If your hand or your foot causes you to sin cut it off and throw it away. It is better for you to enter life maimed or crippled than to have two hands or two feet and be thrown into eternal fire. And if your eye causes you to sin, gouge it out and throw it away. It is better for you to enter life with one eye than to have two eyes and be thrown into the fire of hell. See that you do not look down on one of these little ones. For I tell you that their angels in heaven always see the face of my Father in heaven." -*Matthew 18:1-10*

On the last and greatest day of the Feast, Jesus stood and said in a loud voice, "If anyone is thirsty, let him come to me and drink. Whoever believes in me, as the Scripture has said, streams of living water will flow from within him." -*John 7:37, 38*

You see, at just the right time, when we were still powerless, Christ died for the ungodly.

Very rarely will anyone die for a righteous man, though for a good man someone might possibly dare to die. But God demonstrates his own love for us in this: While we were still sinners, Christ died for us. Since we have now been justified by his blood, how much more shall we be saved from God's wrath through him! For if, when we were God's enemies, we were reconciled to him through the death of his Son, how much more, having been reconciled, shall we be saved through his life! *-Romans 5:6-10*

[So] if you confess with your mouth, "Jesus is Lord," and believe in your heart that God raised him from the dead, you will be saved. For it is with your heart that you believe and are justified, and it is with your mouth that you confess and are saved. *-Romans 10:9,10*

Encourage Your Grandchildren to Love God's Word
I have hidden your word in my heart
that I might not sin against you. . . .
I delight in your decrees;
I will not neglect your word. . . .
Then I will answer the one who taunts me,
for I trust in your word. . . .

My comfort in my suffering is this:
Your promise preserves my life. *-Psalm 119:11, 16, 42, 50*

I remember the days of long ago;
I meditate on all your works
and consider what your hands have done. *-Psalm 143:5*

Your word is a lamp to my feet
and a light for my path. . . .
Sustain me according to your promise,
and I will live; do not let my hopes be dashed. . . .
Direct my footsteps according to your word;
let no sin rule over me. . . .
Your promises have been thoroughly tested,
and your servant loves them. . . .
I rise before dawn and cry for help;
I have put my hope in your word.
My eyes stay open through the watches of the night,
that I may meditate on your promises. . . .

Defend my cause and redeem me;
preserve my life according to your promise.
-Psalm 119:105, 116, 133, 140, 147, 148, 154

Finally, brothers, whatever is true, whatever is noble, whatever is right, whatever is pure, whatever is lovely, whatever is admirable—if anything is excellent or praiseworthy—think about such things. *-Philippians 4:8*

For the word of God is living and active. Sharper than any double-edged sword, it penetrates even to dividing soul and spirit, joints and marrow; it judges the thoughts and attitudes of the heart. Nothing in all creation is hidden from God's sight. Everything is uncovered and laid bare before the eyes of him to whom we must give account.

-Hebrews 4:12, 13

Be diligent in these matters; give yourself wholly to them, so that everyone may see your progress. *-I Timothy 4:15*

All Scripture is God-breathed and is useful for teaching, rebuking, correcting and training in righteousness, so that the man of God may be thoroughly equipped for every good work. *-II Timothy 3:16, 17*

Teach Your Grandchildren to Pray

Let us draw near to God with a sincere heart in full assurance of faith, having our hearts sprinkled to cleanse us from a guilty conscience and having our bodies washed with pure water. *-Hebrews 10:22*

Ask and it will be given to you; seek and you will find; knock and the door will be opened to you. For everyone who asks receives; he who seeks finds; and to him who knocks, the door will be opened.

Which of you, if his son asks for bread, will give him a stone? Or if he asks for a fish, will give him a snake? If you, then, though you are evil, know how to give good gifts to your children, how much more will your Father in heaven give good gifts to those who ask him!

-Matthew 7:7-11

I tell you the truth, whatever you bind on earth will be bound in heaven, and whatever you loose on earth will be loosed in heaven. Again, I tell you that if two of you on earth agree about anything you ask for, it will be done for you by my Father in heaven. For where two or three come together in my name, there am I with them.*-Matthew 18:18-20*

"Have faith in God," Jesus answered. "I tell you the truth, if anyone says to this mountain, 'Go, throw yourself into the sea,' and does not doubt in his heart but believes that what he says will happen, it will be done for him. *-Mark 11:22, 23*

If you remain in me and my words remain in you, ask whatever you wish, and it will be given you. This is to my Father's glory, that you bear much fruit, showing yourselves to be my disciples. As the Father has loved me, so have I loved you. Now remain in my love. If you obey my commands, you will remain in my love, just as I have obeyed my Father's commands and remain in his love. I have told you this so that my joy may be in you and that your joy may be complete. My command is this: Love each other as I have loved you. Greater love has no one than this, that he lay down his life for his friends. You are my friends if you do what I command. I no longer call you servants, because a servant does not know his master's business. Instead, I have called you friends, for everything that I learned from my Father I have made known to you. You did not choose me, but I chose you and appointed you to go and bear fruit—fruit that will last. Then the Father will give you whatever you ask in my name. *-John 15:7-16*

Admit Your Shortcomings to Your Grandchildren

No one lights a lamp and puts it in a place where it will be hidden, or under a bowl. Instead he puts it on its stand, so that those who come in may see the light. Your eye is the lamp of your body. When your eyes are good, your whole body also is full of light. But when they are bad, your body also is full of darkness. See to it, then, that the light within you is not darkness. Therefore, if your whole body is full of light, and no part of it dark, it will be completely lighted, as when the light of a lamp shines on you. *-Luke 11:33-36*

There is nothing concealed that will not be disclosed, or hidden that will not be made known. What you have said in the dark will be heard in the daylight, and what you have whispered in the ear in the inner rooms will be proclaimed from the roofs. *-Luke 12:2, 3*

I know that nothing good lives in me, that is, in my sinful nature. For I have the desire to do what is good, but I cannot carry it out. For what I do is not the good I want to do; no, the evil I do not want to do—this I keep on doing. Now if I do what I do not want to do, it is no longer I who do it, but it is sin living in me that does it. *-Romans 7:18-20*

FOR PERSONAL PRAYER:

Heavenly Father, You have shown me Your desire to give Your blessing to all Your children. May I, too, reach out to young ones seeking to be blessed. Lead me into the words and actions that will convey to them my love and Yours. Amen.

♦ Chapter 5 ♦

'How can I model the kind of home life that glorifies the Lord?'

I think my children and grandchildren need to be reminded that the only sure foundation for a happy home is the Lord Jesus Christ," said Roberto. "I see them working so hard, juggling careers and family, and I admire them for all that effort!

"But I know I can help by being an example of a crucial spiritual truth: No matter how hard we work, we'll still never be able to engineer our own happiness. True and lasting happiness comes only as a result of pursuing the other things: mainly, an awareness of God's guidance, day by day, and a willingness to follow His leading."

FOR MEMORY:
He will be the sure foundation for your times,
a rich store of salvation and wisdom and knowledge;
the fear of the LORD is the key to this treasure.
-*Isaiah 33:6*

FOR SILENT REFLECTION:

♦ *When I was a child, did I sense a reliance on God and His leading in my family? How has that reliance (or lack of it) affected me over the years?*

♦ *In what ways are my children and grandchildren following in my footsteps when it comes to raising their families? What is gratifying to see? What saddens me?*

♦ *How does my own manner of life reflect my desire to serve God each day? In what areas could I seek to strengthen my faith and practical obedience?*

Build Your Own Home on Biblical Foundations:

By wisdom a house is built, and through understanding it is established. -*Proverbs 24:3*

He will be the sure foundation for your times,
a rich store of salvation and wisdom and knowledge;
the fear of the LORD is the key to this treasure. *-Isaiah 33:6*

"Therefore everyone who hears these words of mine and puts them into practice is like a wise man who built his house on the rock. The rain came down, the streams rose, and the winds blew and beat against that house; yet it did not fall, because it had its foundation on the rock. But everyone who hears these words of mine and does not put them into practice is like a foolish man who built his house on sand. The rain came down, the streams rose, and the winds blew and beat against that house, and it fell with a great crash." When Jesus had finished saying these things, the crowds were amazed at his teaching.

-Matthew 7:24-28

It has always been my ambition to preach the gospel where Christ was not known, so that I would not be building on someone else's foundation. *-Romans 15:20*

For no one can lay any foundation other than the one already laid, which is Jesus Christ. If any man builds on this foundation using gold, silver, costly stones, wood, hay or straw, his work will be shown for what it is, because the Day will bring it to light. It will be revealed with fire, and the fire will test the quality of each man's work. If what he has built survives, he will receive his reward. *-I Corinthians 3:11-14*

You also, like living stones, are being built into a spiritual house to be a holy priesthood, offering spiritual sacrifices acceptable to God through Jesus Christ. *-I Peter 2:5*

A Home Where Plans are Based on Eternal Truths

And he told them this parable: "The ground of a certain rich man produced a good crop. He thought to himself, 'What shall I do? I have no place to store my crops.' Then he said, 'This is what I'll do. I will tear down my barns and build bigger ones, and there I will store all my grain and my goods. And I'll say to myself, "You have plenty of good things laid up for many years. Take life easy; eat, drink and be merry." ' But God said to him, 'You fool! This very night your life will be demanded from you. Then who will get what you have prepared for yourself?' This is how it will be with anyone who stores up things for himself but is not rich toward God." *-Luke 12:16-21*

The man who loves his life will lose it,
while the man who hates his life in this world
will keep it for eternal life. *-John 12:25*

Do not deceive yourselves. If any one of you thinks he is wise by the standards of this age, he should become a "fool" so that he may become wise. For the wisdom of this world is foolishness in God's sight. As it is written: "He catches the wise in their craftiness."

-1 Corinthians 3:18, 19

May I never boast except in the cross of our Lord Jesus Christ, through which the world has been crucified to me, and I to the world. *-Galatians 6:14*

The kingdom of the world has become the kingdom of our Lord and of his Christ, and he will reign for ever and ever. *-Revelation 11:15b*

Do not be afraid of those who kill the body but cannot kill the soul. Rather, be afraid of the One who can destroy both soul and body in hell. *-Matthew 10:28*

"There was a rich man who was dressed in purple and fine linen and lived in luxury every day. At his gate was laid a beggar named Lazarus, covered with sores and longing to eat what fell from the rich man's table. Even the dogs came and licked his sores. The time came when the beggar died and the angels carried him to Abraham's side. The rich man also died and was buried. In hell, where he was in torment, he looked up and saw Abraham far away, with Lazarus by his side. So he called to him, 'Father Abraham, have pity on me and send Lazarus to dip the tip of his finger in water and cool my tongue, because I am in agony in this fire.' But Abraham replied, 'Son, remember that in your lifetime you received your good things, while Lazarus received bad things, but now he is comforted here and you are in agony. And besides all this, between us and you a great chasm has been fixed, so that those who want to go from here to you cannot, nor can anyone cross over from there to us.' He answered, 'Then I beg you, father, send Lazarus to my father's house, for I have five brothers. Let him warn them, so that they will not also come to this place of torment.' Abraham replied, 'They have Moses and the Prophets; let them listen to them.' '"No, father Abraham,' he said, 'but if someone from the dead goes to them, they will repent.' He said to him, 'If they do not listen to Moses and the Prophets, they will not be convinced even if someone rises from the dead.' " -*Luke 16:19-31*

A Home Built on God's Greatness

He stood, and shook the earth;
he looked, and made the nations tremble.
The ancient mountains crumbled
and the age-old hills collapsed.
His ways are eternal.

I saw the tents of Cushan in distress,
the dwellings of Midian in anguish.
Were you angry with the rivers, O LORD?
Was your wrath against the streams?
Did you rage against the sea
when you rode with your horses
and your victorious chariots?
You uncovered your bow,
you called for many arrows.
You split the earth with rivers;
the mountains saw you and writhed.
Torrents of water swept by;
the deep roared and lifted its waves on high.
Sun and moon stood still in the heavens
at the glint of your flying arrows,
at the lightning of your flashing spear.
In wrath you strode through the earth
and in anger you threshed the nations.
You came out to deliver your people,

to save your anointed one.
You crushed the leader of the land of wickedness,
you stripped him from head to foot.
With his own spear you pierced his head
when his warriors stormed out to scatter us,
gloating as though about to devour the wretched
who were in hiding.
You trampled the sea with your horses,
churning the great waters. *-Habakkuk 3:6-15*

What, then, shall we say in response to this?
If God is for us, who can be against us? *-Romans 8:31*

A Home Where the Love of God Reigns

So if you faithfully obey the commands I am giving you today—to love the LORD your God and to serve him with all your heart and with all your soul— then I will send rain on your land in its season, both autumn and spring rains, so that you may gather in your grain, new wine and oil. I will provide grass in the fields for your cattle, and you will eat and be satisfied. *-Deuteronomy 11:13-15*

Delight yourself in the LORD
and he will give you the desires of your heart.
-*Psalm 37:4*

The LORD watches over all who love him,
but all the wicked he will destroy. -*Psalm 145:20*

I love those who love me,
and those who seek me find me. -*Proverbs 8:17*

Whoever has my commands and obeys them, he is the one who loves me. He who loves me
will be loved by my Father, and I too will love him and show myself to him."
-*John 14:21*

No eye has seen, no ear has heard, no mind has conceived what God has prepared for
those who love him. -*I Corinthians 2:9b*

Grace to all who love our Lord Jesus Christ with an undying love.
-*Ephesians 6:24*

A Home Where Hospitality Flows

I tell you the truth, anyone who gives you a cup of water in my name because you belong to Christ will certainly not lose his reward. *-Mark 9:41*

"For I was hungry and you gave me something to eat, I was thirsty and you gave me something to drink, I was a stranger and you invited me in, I needed clothes and you clothed me, I was sick and you looked after me, I was in prison and you came to visit me.". . . The King will reply, "I tell you the truth, whatever you did for one of the least of these brothers of mine, you did for me." *-Matthew 25:35, 36,40*

In everything I did, I showed you that by this kind of hard work we must help the weak, remembering the words the Lord Jesus himself said: "It is more blessed to give than to receive." *-Acts 20:35*

Share with God's people who are in need. Practice hospitality. *-Romans 12:13*

Suppose a brother or sister is without clothes and daily food. If one of you says to him, "Go, I wish you well; keep warm and well fed," but does nothing about his physical needs, what good is it? *-James 2:15, 16*

Offer hospitality to one another without grumbling. Each one should use whatever gift he has received to serve others, faithfully administering God's grace in its various forms.
-I Peter 4:9, 10

If anyone has material possessions and sees his brother in need but has no pity on him, how can the love of God be in him? *-I John 3:17*

Do not forget to entertain strangers, for by so doing some people have entertained angels without knowing it. *-Hebrews 13:2*

A Home of Kind Words and Helping Hands

Carry each other's burdens, and in this way you will fulfill the law of Christ. If anyone thinks he is something when he is nothing, he deceives himself. Each one should test his own actions. Then he can take pride in himself, without comparing himself to somebody else. *-Galatians 6:2-4*

Be completely humble and gentle; be patient, bearing with one another in love. Make every effort to keep the unity of the Spirit through the bond of peace. *-Ephesians 4:2, 3*

Speaking the truth in love, we will in all things grow up into him who is the Head, that is, Christ. From him the whole body, joined and held together by every supporting ligament, grows and builds itself up in love, as each part does its work. *-Ephesians 4:15, 16*

Speak to one another with psalms, hymns and spiritual songs. Sing and make music in your heart to the Lord, always giving thanks to God the Father for everything, in the name of our Lord Jesus Christ. *-Ephesians 5:19, 20*

May the God who gives endurance and encouragement give you a spirit of unity among yourselves as you follow Christ Jesus, so that with one heart and mouth you may glorify the God and Father of our Lord Jesus Christ. *-Romans 15:5, 6*

A Home of Lasting Marital Commitment
Enjoy life with your wife, whom you love.
-Ecclesiastes 9:9a

It is God's will that you should be sanctified: that you should avoid sexual immorality.
-1 Thessalonians 4:3

Marriage should be honored by all, and the marriage bed kept pure, for God will judge the adulterer and all the sexually immoral. *-Hebrews 13:4*

Make every effort to live in peace with all men and to be holy; without holiness no one will see the Lord. *-Hebrews 12:14*

To the married I give this command (not I, but the Lord): A wife must not separate from her husband. But if she does, she must remain unmarried or else be reconciled to her husband. And a husband must not divorce his wife. To the rest I say this (I, not the Lord): If any brother has a wife who is not a believer and she is willing to live with him, he must not divorce her. And if a woman has a husband who is not a believer and he is willing to live with her, she must not divorce him. For the unbelieving husband has been sanctified through his wife, and the unbelieving wife has been sanctified through her believing husband. Otherwise your children would be unclean, but as it is, they are holy. But if the unbeliever leaves, let him do so. A believing man or woman is not bound in such circumstances; God has called us to live in peace. How do you know, wife, whether you will save your husband? Or, how do you know, husband, whether you will save your wife?

-I Corinthians 7:10-16

These are those who did not defile themselves with women, for they kept themselves pure. They follow the Lamb wherever he goes. They were purchased from among men and offered as firstfruits to God and the Lamb. *-Revelation 14:4*

Show Grandchildren that God Is Still in Control

The LORD is in his holy temple;
the LORD is on his heavenly throne.
He observes the sons of men;
his eyes examine them. *-Psalm 11:4*

Yours, O LORD, is the greatness and the power
and the glory and the majesty and the splendor,
for everything in heaven and earth is yours.
Yours, O LORD, is the kingdom;
you are exalted as head over all.
Wealth and honor come from you;
you are the ruler of all things.
In your hands are strength and power
to exalt and give strength to all. *-I Chronicles 29:11, 12*

The heavens are yours, and yours also the earth;
you founded the world and all that is in it. *-Psalm 89:11*

I am the LORD, the God of all mankind.
Is anything too hard for me? *-Jeremiah 32:27*

Then Jesus came to them and said, "All authority in heaven
and on earth has been given to me." *-Matthew 28:18*

He Is Sovereign over All

O Sovereign LORD, you have begun to show to your servant your greatness and your strong hand. For what god is there in heaven or on earth who can do the deeds and mighty works you do? *-Deuteronomy 3:24*

"See now that I myself am He! There is no god besides me. I put to death and I bring to life, I have wounded and I will heal, and no one can deliver out of my hand."

-Deuteronomy 32:39

Then the LORD spoke to Job out of the storm:
"Brace yourself like a man;
I will question you, and you shall answer me.
Would you discredit my justice?
Would you condemn me to justify yourself?
Do you have an arm like God's,
and can your voice thunder like his?
Then adorn yourself with glory and splendor,
and clothe yourself in honor and majesty.
Unleash the fury of your wrath,
look at every proud man and bring him low,
look at every proud man and humble him,
crush the wicked where they stand.
Bury them all in the dust together;
shroud their faces in the grave.
Then I myself will admit to you
that your own right hand can save you."
-Job 40:6-14

By wisdom the LORD laid the earth's foundations,
by understanding he set the heavens in place;
by his knowledge the deeps were divided,
and the clouds let drop the dew. -*Proverbs 3:19, 20*

He Is the Ultimate Protector

Hear my cry, O God; listen to my prayer.
From the ends of the earth I call to you,
I call as my heart grows faint;
lead me to the rock that is higher than I.
For you have been my refuge,
a strong tower against the foe.
I long to dwell in your tent forever
and take refuge in the shelter of your wings.
For you have heard my vows, O God;
you have given me the heritage
of those who fear your name.
Increase the days of the king's life,
his years for many generations.

May he be enthroned in God's presence forever;
appoint your love and faithfulness to protect him. *-Psalm 61:1-7*

The LORD is my strength and my shield;
my heart trusts in him, and I am helped.
My heart leaps for joy
and I will give thanks to him in song.
The LORD is the strength of his people,
a fortress of salvation for his anointed one. *-Psalm 28:7, 8*

Do not fret because of evil men
or be envious of those who do wrong;
for like the grass they will soon wither,
like green plants they will soon die away.
Trust in the LORD and do good;
dwell in the land and enjoy safe pasture.
Delight yourself in the LORD
and he will give you the desires of your heart. . . .
Better the little that the righteous have

than the wealth of many wicked; . . .
The days of the blameless are known to the LORD,
and their inheritance will endure forever.
In times of disaster they will not wither;
in days of famine they will enjoy plenty. . . .
If the LORD delights in a man's way,
he makes his steps firm; . . .
They are always generous and lend freely;
their children will be blessed. *-Psalm 37:1-4, 16, 18,19, 23, 26*

He who dwells in the shelter of the Most High
will rest in the shadow of the Almighty.
I will say of the LORD, "He is my refuge and my fortress,
my God, in whom I trust."
Surely he will save you from the fowler's snare
and from the deadly pestilence.
He will cover you with his feathers,
and under his wings you will find refuge;
his faithfulness will be your shield and rampart. *-Psalm 91:1-4*

FOR PERSONAL PRAYER:

Lord, as I survey the story of my life, with all its joys and griefs, I thank You for reminding me that You alone have been in control of my home's happiness. Help me find creative, loving ways to witness to Your ability to build a home on a foundation that lasts. Amen.

♦ Chapter 6 ♦

'What about the times when I feel so isolated?'

It's not as though my children don't care about me," said Ray. "I know they love me, but it's just hard for them to visit much. Their jobs have taken them out of state, and their schedules and parenting responsibilities just don't allow a lot of time off.

"Ever since my wife died, I'm struggling to find a sense of purpose each day. The boredom is starting to get to me, but I know I can't depend on my children to entertain me. They're here once or twice a year, and it's great. But the rest of the time it's up to me to carve out a new kind of life for myself."

> ### FOR MEMORY:
> Even to your old age and gray hairs I am he,
> I am he who will sustain you.
> I have made you and I will carry you;
> I will sustain you and I will rescue you.
> *-Isaiah 46:4*

FOR SILENT REFLECTION:

◆ *In what ways am I having to modify my expectations about my life and goals lately? How hard is this for me? What are the joys and the griefs behind these changes?*

◆ *What new ways of reaching out to others have I considered?*

◆ *Have I checked into the possibility of volunteer work in my community? What about the opportunities for fellowship in my church?*

◆ *How can I increase my awareness of God's presence when I'm feeling lonely or left out? What Scripture passages might be good to meditate on today?*

Coping with the Possibility of Loneliness or Isolation?

Though my father and mother forsake me, the LORD will receive me. *-Psalm 27:10*

For the LORD will not reject his people;
he will never forsake his inheritance. *-Psalm 94:14*

I, the LORD, have called you in righteousness;
I will take hold of your hand.
I will keep you and will make you to be a covenant
for the people and a light for the Gentiles. *-Isaiah 42:6*

"Though the mountains be shaken and the hills be removed,
yet my unfailing love for you will not be shaken
nor my covenant of peace be removed,"
says the LORD, who has compassion on you. *-Isaiah 54:10*

Keep your lives free from the love of money
and be content with what you have,
because God has said,
"Never will I leave you;
never will I forsake you." *-Hebrews 13:5*

Feeling Discouraged or Depressed?

My tears have been my food day and night,
while men say to me all day long, "Where is your God? -*Psalm 42:3*

Record my lament; list my tears on your scroll—
are they not in your record? -*Psalm 56:8*

The churning inside me never stops;
days of suffering confront me. -*Job 30:27*

I am feeble and utterly crushed;
I groan in anguish of heart.
All my longings lie open before you, O Lord;
my sighing is not hidden from you.
My heart pounds, my strength fails me;
even the light has gone from my eyes.
My friends and companions avoid me because of my wounds;
my neighbors stay far away. -*Psalm 38:8-11*

For my days vanish like smoke;
my bones burn like glowing embers.
My heart is blighted and withered like grass;
I forget to eat my food.
Because of my loud groaning
I am reduced to skin and bones.
I am like a desert owl,
like an owl among the ruins.
I lie awake;
I have become like a bird alone on a roof.
All day long my enemies taunt me;
those who rail against me use my name as a curse.
For I eat ashes as my food
and mingle my drink with tears
because of your great wrath,
for you have taken me up and thrown me aside.
My days are like the evening shadow;
I wither away like grass.
-Psalm 102:3-11

Hear my prayer, O LORD,
listen to my cry for help; be not deaf to my weeping.
For I dwell with you as an alien,
a stranger, as all my fathers were. *-Psalm 39:12*

God Offers Comfort When You Cry

Those who sow in tears
will reap with songs of joy. *-Psalm 126:5*

This is what the LORD says: "Restrain your voice from weeping and your eyes from
tears, for your work will be rewarded," declares the LORD. *-Jeremiah 31:16a*

The sorrows for the appointed feasts I will remove from you;
they are a burden and a reproach to you. *-Zephaniah 3:18*

I tell you the truth, you will weep and mourn while the world rejoices. You will grieve,
but your grief will turn to joy. A woman giving birth to a child has pain because her time
has come; but when her baby is born she forgets the anguish because of her joy that a
child is born into the world. *-John 16:20-21*

During the days of Jesus' life on earth, he offered up prayers and petitions with loud cries and tears to the one who could save him from death, and he was heard because of his reverent submission. *-Hebrews 5:7*

And I heard a loud voice from the throne saying, "Now the dwelling of God is with men, and he will live with them. They will be his people, and God himself will be with them and be their God. He will wipe every tear from their eyes. There will be no more death or mourning or crying or pain, for the old order of things has passed away." *-Revelation 21:3, 4*

You Can Rely upon God in Depression

But you, O God, do see trouble and grief;
  you consider it to take it in hand.
The victim commits himself to you;
  you are the helper of the fatherless.
  -Psalm 10:14

My flesh and my heart may fail,
  but God is the strength of my heart
and my portion forever. *-Psalm 73:26*

Unless the LORD had given me help,
I would soon have dwelt in the silence of death.
When I said, "My foot is slipping,"
your love, O LORD, supported me.
When anxiety was great within me,
your consolation brought joy to my soul. *-Psalm 94:17-19*

The Sovereign LORD has given me an instructed tongue,
to know the word that sustains the weary.
He wakens me morning by morning,
wakens my ear to listen like one being taught.
The Sovereign LORD has opened my ears,
and I have not been rebellious;
I have not drawn back.
I offered my back to those who beat me,
my cheeks to those who pulled out my beard;
I did not hide my face from mocking and spitting.
Because the Sovereign LORD helps me, I will not be disgraced.
Therefore have I set my face like flint,

and I know I will not be put to shame.
He who vindicates me is near.
Who then will bring charges against me?
Let us face each other!
Who is my accuser? Let him confront me!
It is the Sovereign LORD who helps me.
Who is he that will condemn me?
They will all wear out like a garment; the moths will eat them up.
Who among you fears the LORD and obeys the word of his servant?
Let him who walks in the dark, who has no light,
trust in the name of the LORD and rely on his God. *-Isaiah 50:4-10*

Come to me, all you who are weary and burdened, and I will give you rest. Take my yoke upon you and learn from me, for I am gentle and humble in heart, and you will find rest for your souls. For my yoke is easy and my burden is light. *-Matthew 11:28-30*

Do not let your hearts be troubled. Trust in God; trust also in me. . . . Peace I leave with you; my peace I give you. I do not give to you as the world gives. Do not let your hearts be troubled and do not be afraid. *-John 14:1, 27*

We are hard pressed on every side, but not crushed; perplexed, but not in despair; persecuted, but not abandoned; struck down, but not destroyed. . . . Therefore we do not lose heart. Though outwardly we are wasting away, yet inwardly we are being renewed day by day. For our light and momentary troubles are achieving for us an eternal glory that far outweighs them all. So we fix our eyes not on what is seen, but on what is unseen. For what is seen is temporary, but what is unseen is eternal. *-II Corinthians 4:8, 9, 16-18*

For the grace of God that brings salvation has appeared to all men. It teaches us to say "No" to ungodliness and worldly passions, and to live self-controlled, upright and godly lives in this present age, while we wait for the blessed hope—the glorious appearing of our great God and Savior, Jesus Christ, who gave himself for us to redeem us from all wickedness and to purify for himself a people that are his very own, eager to do what is good. *-Titus 2:11-14*

In this you greatly rejoice, though now for a little
while you may have had to suffer grief in all kinds of trials.
-I Peter 1:6

Facing Loss as You Grow Older?

Cast your cares on the LORD and he will sustain you;
he will never let the righteous fall. *-Psalm 55:22*

And I will ask the Father, and he will give you another Counselor to be with you forever— the Spirit of truth. The world cannot accept him, because it neither sees him nor knows him. But you know him, for he lives with you and will be in you. I will not leave you as orphans; I will come to you. Before long, the world will not see me anymore, but you will see me. Because I live, you also will live. . . .

Peace I leave with you; my peace I give you. I do not give to you as the world gives. Do not let your hearts be troubled and do not be afraid. *-John 14:16-19, 27*

Therefore, brothers, since we have confidence to enter the Most Holy Place by the blood of Jesus, by a new and living way opened for us through the curtain, that is, his body, and since we have a great priest over the house of God, let us draw near to God with a sincere heart in full assurance of faith, having our hearts sprinkled to cleanse us from a guilty conscience and having our bodies washed with pure water.

-Hebrews 10:19-22

In this way, love is made complete among us so that we will have confidence on the day of judgment, because in this world we are like him. There is no fear in love. But perfect love drives out fear, because fear has to do with punishment. The one who fears is not made perfect in love. *-1 John 4:17, 18*

Loss of a Spouse through Death

Sarah lived to be a hundred and twenty-seven years old. She died at Kiriath Arba (that is, Hebron) in the land of Canaan, and Abraham went to mourn for Sarah and to weep over her. Then Abraham rose from beside his dead wife and spoke to the Hittites. He said, "I am an alien and a stranger among you. Sell me some property for a burial site here so I can bury my dead." The Hittites replied to Abraham, "Sir, listen to us. You are a mighty prince among us. Bury your dead in the choicest of our tombs. None of us will refuse you his tomb for burying your dead." Then Abraham rose and bowed down before the people of the land, the Hittites. *-Genesis 23:1-7*

In the days when the judges ruled, there was a famine in the land, and a man from Bethlehem in Judah, together with his wife and two sons, went to live for a while in the country of Moab. The man's name was Elimelech, his wife's name Naomi, and the names of his two sons were Mahlon and Kilion. They were Ephrathites from Bethlehem, Judah.

And they went to Moab and lived there. Now Elimelech, Naomi's husband, died, and she was left with her two sons. They married Moabite women, one named Orpah and the other Ruth. After they had lived there about ten years, both Mahlon and Kilion also died, and Naomi was left without her two sons and her husband. *-Ruth 1:1-5*

Loss of a Spouse through Divorce

"I hate divorce," says the LORD God of Israel, "and I hate a man's covering himself with violence as well as with his garment," says the LORD Almighty. So guard yourself in your spirit, and do not break faith. *-Malachi 2:16*

It has been said, "Anyone who divorces his wife must give her a certificate of divorce." But I tell you that anyone who divorces his wife, except for marital unfaithfulness, causes her to become an adulteress, and anyone who marries the divorced woman commits adultery. *-Matthew 5:31, 32*

Some Pharisees came to him to test him. They asked, "Is it lawful for a man to divorce his wife for any and every reason?" . . . "Why then," they asked, "did Moses command that a man give his wife a certificate of divorce and send her away?" Jesus replied, "Moses permitted you to divorce your wives because your hearts were hard. But it was not this way from the beginning. I tell you that anyone who divorces his wife, except for marital unfaithfulness, and marries another woman commits adultery." -*Matthew 19:3,7-9*

Some Pharisees came and tested him by asking, "Is it lawful for a man to divorce his wife?" "What did Moses command you?" he replied. They said, "Moses permitted a man to write a certificate of divorce and send her away." "It was because your hearts were hard that Moses wrote you this law," Jesus replied. "But at the beginning of creation God 'made them male and female.' 'For this reason a man will leave his father and mother and be united to his wife, and the two will become one flesh.' So they are no longer two, but one. Therefore what God has joined together, let man not separate." When they were in the house again, the disciples asked Jesus about this. He answered, "Anyone who divorces his wife and marries another woman commits adultery against her. And if she divorces her husband and marries another man, she commits adultery." -*Mark 10:2-12*

> Are you married? Do not seek a divorce.
> Are you unmarried? Do not look for a wife.
> -*1 Corinthians 7:27*

God Calls You to Persevere in the Midst of Loss

But mark this: There will be terrible times in the last days. People will be lovers of themselves, lovers of money, boastful, proud, abusive, disobedient to their parents, ungrateful, unholy, without love, unforgiving, slanderous, without self-control, brutal, not lovers of the good, treacherous, rash, conceited, lovers of pleasure rather than lovers of God. *-II Timothy 3:1-4*

Therefore, prepare your minds for action; be self-controlled; set your hope fully on the grace to be given you when Jesus Christ is revealed. As obedient children, do not conform to the evil desires you had when you lived in ignorance. But just as he who called you is holy, so be holy in all you do; for it is written: "Be holy, because I am holy."

-I Peter 1:13-16

Anyone who does not carry his cross and follow me cannot be my disciple. Suppose one of you wants to build a tower. Will he not first sit down and estimate the cost to see if he has enough money to complete it? For if he lays the foundation and is not able to finish it, everyone who sees it will ridicule him, saying, "This fellow began to build and was not able to finish." Or suppose a king is about to go to war against another king. Will he not first sit down and consider whether he is able with ten thousand men to oppose the one coming against him with twenty thousand? If he is not able, he will send a delegation while the other is still a long way off and will ask for terms of peace. In the same way, any of you who does not give up everything he has cannot be my disciple.

Salt is good, but if it loses its saltiness, how can it be made salty again? It is fit neither for the soil nor for the manure pile; it is thrown out. He who has ears to hear, let him hear. *-Luke 14:27-35*

Yet I am not ashamed, because I know whom I have believed, and am convinced that he is able to guard what I have entrusted to him for that day. *-II Timothy 1:12b*

Explore New Avenues of Friendship

How good and pleasant it is
when brothers live together in unity!
It is like precious oil poured on the head, running down on the beard,
running down on Aaron's beard, down upon the collar of his robes.
It is as if the dew of Hermon were falling on Mount Zion.
For there the LORD bestows his blessing,
even life forevermore. *-Psalm 133:1-3*

When Job's three friends, Eliphaz the Temanite, Bildad the Shuhite and Zophar the Naamathite, heard about all the troubles that had come upon him, they set out from their homes and met together by agreement to go and sympathize with him and comfort him. When they saw him from a distance, they could hardly recognize him; they began to weep aloud, and they tore their robes and sprinkled dust on their heads. Then they sat on the ground with him for seven days and seven nights. No one said a word to him, because they saw how great his suffering was. *-Job 2:11-13*

Be devoted to one another in brotherly love.
Honor one another above yourselves. *-Romans 12:10*

Therefore encourage one another and build each other up, just as in fact you are doing. . . . And we urge you, brothers, warn those who are idle, encourage the timid, help the weak, be patient with everyone. *-1 Thessalonians 5:11, 14*

Therefore encourage each other with these words. *-1 Thessalonians 4:18*

Find Support in Church Fellowship

Let us not give up meeting together, as some are in the habit of doing, but let us encourage one another—and all the more as you see the Day approaching. *-Hebrews 10:25*

The body is a unit, though it is made up of many parts; and though all its parts are many, they form one body. So it is with Christ. For we were all baptized by one Spirit into one body—whether Jews or Greeks, slave or free—and we were all given the one Spirit to drink.

Now the body is not made up of one part but of many. If the foot should say, "Because I am not a hand, I do not belong to the body," it would not for that reason cease to be part of the body. And if the ear should say, "Because I am not an eye, I do not belong to the body," it would not for that reason cease to be part of the body. If the whole body were an eye, where would the sense of hearing be? If the whole body were an ear, where would the sense of smell be?

But in fact God has arranged the parts in the body, every one of them, just as he wanted them to be. If they were all one part, where would the body be? As it is, there are many parts, but one body. The eye cannot say to the hand, "I don't need you!" And the head cannot say to the feet, "I don't need you!"

121

On the contrary, those parts of the body that seem to be weaker are indispensable, and the parts that we think are less honorable we treat with special honor. And the parts that are unpresentable are treated with special modesty, while our presentable parts need no special treatment. But God has combined the members of the body and has given greater honor to the parts that lacked it, so that there should be no division in the body, but that its parts should have equal concern for each other.

If one part suffers, every part suffers with it; if one part is honored, every part rejoices with it. *-I Corinthians 12:12-26*

They devoted themselves to the apostles' teaching and to the fellowship, to the breaking of bread and to prayer. Everyone was filled with awe, and many wonders and miraculous signs were done by the apostles. All the believers were together and had everything in common. Selling their possessions and goods, they gave to anyone as he had need. Every day they continued to meet together in the temple courts. They broke bread in their homes and ate together with glad and sincere hearts, praising God and enjoying the favor of all the people. And the Lord added to their number daily those who were being saved.

-Acts 2:42-47

There is one body and one Spirit—just as you were called to one hope when you were called—one Lord, one faith, one baptism; one God and Father of all, who is over all and through all and in all. *-Ephesians 4:4-6*

If anyone says, "I love God," yet hates his brother, he is a liar. For anyone who does not love his brother, whom he has seen, cannot love God, whom he has not seen. And he has given us this command: Whoever loves God must also love his brother.

-I John 4:20, 21

FOR PERSONAL PRAYER:

Father, thank You for the promises of Your constant presence. May I experience the fulfillment of those promises in practical ways every day. I need to know what it means, right now, that You are near me. Amen.

♦ Chapter 7 ♦

'How shall I deal with the rebellion of my adult children?'

I feel I'm worthy of their respect," said Willena. "But two of my children just haven't turned out the way I had hoped. They refuse to listen to anything I suggest—ways they could start to get themselves out of the trouble they're in.

"I can't think of anything harder for a parent and grandparent than to see their children grow up to be rebellious and dishonest as adults. What's worse, they seem to spurn every bit of moral teaching we've tried to instill. But I won't give up on them; I know God cares about them even more than I do. I keep praying for a breakthrough."

FOR MEMORY:

Teach the older men to be temperate, worthy of respect, self-controlled, and sound in faith, in love and in endurance. Likewise, teach the older women to be reverent in the way they live, not to be slanderers or addicted to much wine, but to teach what is good.

-Titus 2:2, 3

FOR SILENT REFLECTION:

♦ *What forms of rebellion did I express with my own parents and grandparents? What effect did this have on them and me? How have things changed since then?*

♦ *What things about the lives of my adult children please me? sadden me?*

♦ *To what extent am I willing to let my adult children take responsibility for their own lives? In what areas do I still have a chance to influence them for the good?*

♦ *How can I pray today for my adult children and their children?*

Fighting with Rebellious Adult Children?

The acts of the sinful nature are obvious: sexual immorality, impurity and debauchery; idolatry and witchcraft; hatred, discord, jealousy, fits of rage, selfish ambition, dissensions, factions and envy; drunkenness, orgies, and the like. I warn you, as I did before, that those who live like this will not inherit the kingdom of God. *-Galatians 5:19-21*

If anyone thinks he is something when he is nothing, he deceives himself. Each one should test his own actions. Then he can take pride in himself, without comparing himself to somebody else, for each one should carry his own load. *-Galatians 6:3-5*

If we claim to be without sin, we deceive ourselves and the truth is not in us. If we confess our sins, he is faithful and just and will forgive us our sins and purify us from all unrighteousness. *-I John 1:8, 9*

The Pain of an Adult Child Gone Wrong

While they were on their way, the report came to David: "Absalom has struck down all the king's sons; not one of them is left." The king stood up, tore his clothes and lay down on the ground; and all his servants stood by with their clothes torn. . . .

Meanwhile, Absalom had fled. *-II Samuel 13:30, 31, 34a*

Absalom lived two years in Jerusalem without seeing the king's face. . . .

In the course of time, Absalom provided himself with a chariot and horses and with fifty men to run ahead of him. . . .

A messenger came and told David, "The hearts of the men of Israel are with Absalom." Then David said to all his officials who were with him in Jerusalem, "Come! We must flee, or none of us will escape from Absalom. We must leave immediately, or he will move quickly to overtake us and bring ruin upon us and put the city to the sword."

-II Samuel 14:28; 15:1, 13, 14

Joab said, "I'm not going to wait like this for you." So he took three javelins in his hand and plunged them into Absalom's heart while Absalom was still alive in the oak tree. . .

Then the Cushite arrived and said, "My lord the king, hear the good news! The LORD has delivered you today from all who rose up against you." The king asked the Cushite, "Is the young man Absalom safe?" The Cushite replied, "May the enemies of my lord the king and all who rise up to harm you be like that young man."

The king was shaken. He went up to the room over the gateway and wept. As he went, he said: "O my son Absalom! My son, my son Absalom! If only I had died instead of you—O Absalom, my son, my son!" Joab was told, "The king is weeping and mourning for Absalom." And for the whole army the victory that day was turned into mourning, because on that day the troops heard it said, "The king is grieving for his son." The men stole into the city that day as men steal in who are ashamed when they flee from battle.

The king covered his face and cried aloud, "O my son Absalom! O Absalom, my son, my son!" -II Samuel 18:14, 31-33; 19:1-4

The Sons of Korah and Eliab Challenge Authority

Korah son of Izhar, the son of Kohath, the son of Levi, and certain Reubenites—Dathan and Abiram, sons of Eliab, and On son of Peleth—became insolent and rose up against Moses. With them were 250 Israelite men, well-known community leaders who had been appointed members of the council. They came as a group to oppose Moses and Aaron and said to them, "You have gone too far! The whole community is holy, every one of them, and the LORD is with them. Why then do you set yourselves above the LORD'S assembly?" When Moses heard this, he fell facedown. . . .

Then Moses summoned Dathan and Abiram, the sons of Eliab. But they said, "We will not come! Isn't it enough that you have brought us up out of a land flowing with milk and honey to kill us in the desert? And now you also want to lord it over us? Moreover, you haven't brought us into a land flowing with milk and honey or given us an inheritance of fields and vineyards. Will you gouge out the eyes of these men? No, we will not come!" Then Moses became very angry and said to the LORD, "Do not accept their offering. I have not taken so much as a donkey from them, nor have I wronged any of them." -Numbers 16:1-4, 12-15

Eli's Sons Just Won't Listen

Eli's sons were wicked men; they had no regard for the LORD. Now it was the practice of the priests with the people that whenever anyone offered a sacrifice and while the meat was being boiled, the servant of the priest would come with a three-pronged fork in his hand. He would plunge it into the pan or kettle or caldron or pot, and the priest would take for himself whatever the fork brought up. This is how they treated all the Israelites who came to Shiloh. But even before the fat was burned, the servant of the priest would come and say to the man who was sacrificing, "Give the priest some meat to roast; he won't accept boiled meat from you, but only raw." If the man said to him, "Let the fat be burned up first, and then take whatever you want," the servant would then answer, "No, hand it over now; if you don't, I'll take it by force." This sin of the young men was very great in the LORD'S sight, for they were treating the LORD'S offering with contempt. . . .

Now Eli, who was very old, heard about everything his sons were doing to all Israel and how they slept with the women who served at the entrance to the Tent of Meeting. So he said to them, "Why do you do such things? I hear from all the people about these wicked deeds of yours. No, my sons; it is not a good report that I hear spreading among the LORD'S people. If a man sins against another man, God may mediate for him; but if a man sins against the LORD, who will intercede for him?" His sons, however, did not listen to their father's rebuke. *-I Samuel 2:12-17, 22-25*

♦ Assure Them of Acceptance When They Return ♦

A Son Wants Out

There was a man who had two sons. The younger one said to his father, "Father, give me my share of the estate." So he divided his property between them. Not long after that, the younger son got together all he had, set off for a distant country and there squandered his wealth in wild living. *-Luke 15:11b-13*

He Suffers, then Sees His Error

After he had spent everything, there was a severe famine in that whole country, and he began to be in need. So he went and hired himself out to a citizen of that country, who sent him to his fields to feed pigs. He longed to fill his stomach with the pods that the pigs were eating, but no one gave him anything. When he came to his senses, he said, "How many of my father's hired men have food to spare, and here I am starving to death! I will set out and go back to my father and say to him: Father, I have sinned against heaven and against you. I am no longer worthy to be called your son; make me like one of your hired men." *-Luke 15:14-19*

His Father Accepts Him Back

So he got up and went to his father. But while he was still a long way off, his father saw him and was filled with compassion for him; he ran to his son, threw his arms around him and kissed him. The son said to him, "Father, I have sinned against heaven and against you. I am no longer worthy to be called your son."

But the father said to his servants, "Quick! Bring the best robe and put it on him. Put a ring on his finger and sandals on his feet. Bring the fattened calf and kill it. Let's have a feast and celebrate. For this son of mine was dead and is alive again; he was lost and is found." So they began to celebrate. *-Luke 15:20-24*

With God's Help, the Rebellious Can Change

Blessed is the man whom God corrects;
so do not despise the discipline of the Almighty.
For he wounds, but he also binds up;
he injures, but his hands also heal.
From six calamities he will rescue you;
in seven no harm will befall you.
In famine he will ransom you from death,
and in battle from the stroke of the sword.

You will be protected from the lash of the tongue,
and need not fear when destruction comes.
You will laugh at destruction and famine,
and need not fear the beasts of the earth.
For you will have a covenant with the stones of the field,
and the wild animals will be at peace with you.
You will know that your tent is secure;
you will take stock of your property and find nothing missing.
You will know that your children will be many,
and your descendants like the grass of the earth.
You will come to the grave in full vigor,
like sheaves gathered in season. *-Job 5:17-26*

Good and upright is the LORD;
therefore he instructs sinners in his ways.
He guides the humble in what is right
and teaches them his way.
All the ways of the LORD are loving and faithful
for those who keep the demands of his covenant.

For the sake of your name, O LORD,
forgive my iniquity, though it is great. *-Psalm 25:8-11*

A man who remains stiff-necked after many rebukes
will suddenly be destroyed—without remedy. . . .
A man's pride brings him low,
but a man of lowly spirit gains honor. *-Proverbs 29:1, 23*

And you have forgotten that word of encouragement that addresses you as sons: "My son, do not make light of the Lord's discipline, and do not lose heart when he rebukes you, because the Lord disciplines those he loves, and he punishes everyone he accepts as a son." Endure hardship as discipline; God is treating you as sons. For what son is not disciplined by his father? If you are not disciplined (and everyone undergoes discipline), then you are illegitimate children and not true sons. Moreover, we have all had human fathers who disciplined us and we respected them for it. How much more should we submit to the Father of our spirits and live! *-Hebrews 12:5-9*

Extend Mercy in God's Strength
He who conceals his sins does not prosper,
but whoever confesses and renounces them finds mercy. *-Proverbs 28:13*

133

Yet the LORD longs to be gracious to you;
he rises to show you compassion.
For the LORD is a God of justice.
Blessed are all who wait for him! *-Isaiah 30:18*

As a father has compassion on his children,
so the LORD has compassion on those who fear him . . . .
But from everlasting to everlasting
the LORD'S love is with those who fear him,
and his righteousness with their children's children— *-Psalm 103:13, 17*

Praise the LORD, O my soul,
and forget not all his benefits—
who forgives all your sins
and heals all your diseases,
who redeems your life from the pit
and crowns you with love and compassion,
who satisfies your desires with good things
so that your youth is renewed like the eagle's. *-Psalm 103:2-5*

It is good for a man to bear the yoke while he is young.
Let him sit alone in silence, for the LORD has laid it on him.
Let him bury his face in the dust—there may yet be hope.
Let him offer his cheek to one who would strike him,
and let him be filled with disgrace.
For men are not cast off by the Lord forever.
Though he brings grief, he will show compassion,
so great is his unfailing love.
For he does not willingly bring affliction
or grief to the children of men. *-Lamentations 3:27-33*

Offer Forgiveness, as God Has Forgiven You
Forgive us our debts,
as we also have forgiven our debtors. *-Matthew 6:12*

Blessed is he whose transgressions are forgiven,
whose sins are covered.
Blessed is the man whose sin the LORD does not count against him
and in whose spirit there is no deceit.

When I kept silent, my bones wasted away
through my groaning all day long.
For day and night your hand was heavy upon me;
my strength was sapped as in the heat of summer.
Then I acknowledged my sin to you
and did not cover up my iniquity.
I said, "I will confess my transgressions to the LORD"—
and you forgave the guilt of my sin.
Therefore let everyone who is godly
pray to you while you may be found;
surely when the mighty waters rise, they will not reach him.
You are my hiding place; you will protect me from trouble
and surround me with songs of deliverance.
I will instruct you and teach you
in the way you should go;
I will counsel you and watch over you.
-Psalm 32:1, 6-8

Offer Godly Intstruction to Your Granchildren

Only be careful, and watch yourselves closely so that you do not forget the things your eyes have seen or let them slip from your heart as long as you live. Teach them to your children and to their children after them. Remember the day you stood before the LORD your God at Horeb, when he said to me, "Assemble the people before me to hear my words so that they may learn to revere me as long as they live in the land and may teach them to their children." *-Deuteronomy 4:9, 10*

These commandments that I give you today are to be upon your hearts. Impress them on your children. Talk about them when you sit at home and when you walk along the road, when you lie down and when you get up. Tie them as symbols on your hands and bind them on your foreheads. Write them on the doorframes of your houses and on your gates.
-Deuteronomy 6:6-9

Teach them to your children, talking about them when you sit at home and when you walk along the road, when you lie down and when you get up. *-Deuteronomy 11:19*

I will open my mouth in parables,
I will utter hidden things, things from of old—what we have heard and known,
what our fathers have told us.

We will not hide them from their children;
we will tell the next generation
the praiseworthy deeds of the LORD,
his power, and the wonders he has done. *-Psalm 78:2-4*

Discipline your son,
and he will give you peace;
he will bring delight to your soul. *-Proverbs 29:17*

He who spares the rod hates his son,
but he who loves him is careful to discipline him. *-Proverbs 13:24*

If you, then, though you are evil, know how to give good gifts to your children, how much more will your Father in heaven give good gifts to those who ask him!
-Matthew 7:11

[A church leader] must manage his own family well and see that his children obey him with proper respect. (If anyone does not know how to manage his own family, how can he take care of God's church?) He must not be a recent convert, or he may become conceited and fall under the same judgment as the devil. He must also have a good reputation with outsiders, so that he will not fall into disgrace and into the devil's trap. Deacons, likewise, are to be men worthy of respect, sincere, not indulging in much wine, and not pursuing dishonest gain. They must keep hold of the deep truths of the faith with a clear conscience. They must first be tested; and then if there is nothing against them, let them serve as deacons. In the same way, their wives are to be women worthy of respect, not malicious talkers but temperate and trustworthy in everything. A deacon must be the husband of but one wife and must manage his children and his household well. *-1 Timothy 3:4-12*

Help Them Learn Respect for Their Parents

Honor your father and your mother, as the LORD your God has commanded you, so that you may live long and that it may go well with you in the land the LORD your God is giving you. *-Deuteronomy 5:16*

> Children, obey your parents in everything,
> for this pleases the Lord. *-Colossians 3:20*

139

My son, if your heart is wise,
then my heart will be glad;
my inmost being will rejoice
when your lips speak what is right. . . .
Listen to your father, who gave you life,
and do not despise your mother when she is old. . . .
The father of a righteous man has great joy;
he who has a wise son delights in him.
May your father and mother be glad;
may she who gave you birth rejoice!
My son, give me your heart
and let your eyes keep to my ways. -*Proverbs 23:15, 16, 22, 24-26*

Help Them Learn to Delay Gratification

He who loves pleasure will become poor;
whoever loves wine and oil will never be rich. -*Proverbs 21:17*

But mark this: There will be terrible times in the last days. People will be lovers of them-selves, lovers of money, boastful, proud, abusive, disobedient to their parents, ungrateful, unholy, without love, unforgiving, slanderous, without self-control, brutal, not lovers of the good, treacherous, rash, conceited, lovers of pleasure rather than lovers of God.

-II Timothy 3:1-4

Therefore, prepare your minds for action; be self-controlled; set your hope fully on the grace to be given you when Jesus Christ is revealed. As obedient children, do not conform to the evil desires you had when you lived in ignorance. But just as he who called you is holy, so be holy in all you do; for it is written: "Be holy, because I am holy."

-I Peter 1:13-16

Anyone who does not carry his cross and follow me cannot be my disciple. Suppose one of you wants to build a tower. Will he not first sit down and estimate the cost to see if he has enough money to complete it? For if he lays the foundation and is not able to finish it, everyone who sees it will ridicule him, saying, "This fellow began to build and was not able to finish." Or suppose a king is about to go to war against another king. Will he not first sit down and consider whether he is able with ten thousand men to oppose the one coming against him with twenty thousand? If he is not able, he will send a delegation while the other is still a long way off and will ask for terms of peace. In the same way, any of you who does not give up everything he has cannot be my disciple.

Salt is good, but if it loses its saltiness, how can it be made salty again? It is fit neither for the soil nor for the manure pile; it is thrown out. He who has ears to hear, let him hear. *-Luke 14:27-35*

That is why I am suffering as I am. Yet I am not ashamed, because I know whom I have believed, and am convinced that he is able to guard what I have entrusted to him for that day. *- II Timothy 1:12*

Help Them Resist Their Temptations

No temptation has seized you except what is common to man. And God is faithful; he will not let you be tempted beyond what you can bear. But when you are tempted, he will also provide a way out so that you can stand up under it. *- I Corinthians 10:13*

Finally, be strong in the Lord and in his mighty power. Put on the full armor of God so that you can take your stand against the devil's schemes. For our struggle is not against flesh and blood, but against the rulers, against the authorities, against the powers of this dark world and against the spiritual forces of evil in the heavenly realms. Therefore put on the full armor of God, so that when the day of evil comes, you may be able to stand your ground, and after you have done everything, to stand. Stand firm then, with the belt of truth buckled around your waist, with the breastplate of righteousness in place, and with your feet fitted with the readiness that comes from the gospel of peace. In addition to all this, take up the shield of faith, with which you can extinguish all the flaming arrows of the evil one. Take the helmet of salvation and the sword of the Spirit, which is the word of God. And pray in the Spirit on all occasions with all kinds of prayers and requests. With this in mind, be alert and always keep on praying for all the saints.

-Ephesians 6:10-18

But the Lord is faithful, and he will strengthen and protect you from the evil one.

-II Thessalonians 3:3

Be self-controlled and alert. Your enemy the devil prowls around like a roaring lion looking for someone to devour. Resist him, standing firm in the faith, because you know that your brothers throughout the world are undergoing the same kind of sufferings. And the God of all grace, who called you to his eternal glory in Christ, after you have suffered a little while, will himself restore you and make you strong, firm and steadfast.

-I Peter 5:8-10

Help Them Make Good Life-style Choices

This day I call heaven and earth as witnesses against you that I have set before you life and death, blessings and curses. Now choose life, so that you and your children may live.

-Deuteronomy 30:19

But if serving the LORD seems undesirable to you, then choose for yourselves this day whom you will serve, whether the gods your forefathers served beyond the River, or the gods of the Amorites, in whose land you are living. But as for me and my household, we will serve the LORD." *-Joshua 24:15*

"Not everyone who says to me, 'Lord, Lord,' will enter the kingdom of heaven, but only he who does the will of my Father who is in heaven. Many will say to me on that day, 'Lord, Lord, did we not prophesy in your name, and in your name drive out demons and perform many miracles?' Then I will tell them plainly, 'I never knew you. Away from me, you evildoers!' Therefore everyone who hears these words of mine and puts them into practice is like a wise man who built his house on the rock. The rain came down, the streams rose, and the winds blew and beat against that house; yet it did not fall, because it had its foundation on the rock. But everyone who hears these words of mine and does not put them into practice is like a foolish man who built his house on sand. The rain came down, the streams rose, and the winds blew and beat against that house, and it fell with a great crash." When Jesus had finished saying these things, the crowds were amazed at his teaching. *-Matthew 7:21-28*

Do not merely listen to the word, and so deceive yourselves. Do what it says. Anyone who listens to the word but does not do what it says is like a man who looks at his face in a mirror and, after looking at himself, goes away and immediately forgets what he looks like. But the man who looks intently into the perfect law that gives freedom, and continues to do this, not forgetting what he has heard, but doing it—he will be blessed in what he does. If anyone considers himself religious and yet does not keep a tight rein on his tongue, he deceives himself and his religion is worthless. Religion that God our Father accepts as pure and faultless is this: to look after orphans and widows in their distress and to keep oneself from being polluted by the world. *-James 1:22-27*

FOR PERSONAL PRAYER:

Lord Jesus, I am grieved by some of the things my children and grandchildren do. Help me to keep loving them with the same kind of unconditional love that You have extended to me. Keep me faithful as I seek Your strength and patience to meet all trials. Amen.

♦ Chapter 8 ♦

'How can I stay aware of my life's ultimate destination?'

I think as I get older I'm becoming a little more aware of my own mortality," said Jared. "When I was younger I suppose I thought I'd live forever, never giving a thought to the idea of eternal destiny. But my health has suffered a bit lately, and I'm realizing how fragile life can be.

"Of course, all of this is really true of anyone—no matter what their age. In a sense all of us, from the moment of birth, are just one heartbeat away from eternity."

FOR MEMORY:
I know that my Redeemer lives,
and that in the end he will stand upon the earth.
And after my skin has been destroyed, yet in my flesh I will see God.
-Job 19:25, 26

FOR SILENT REFLECTION:

♦ *What was I taught by my parents about human mortality and eternity?*

♦ *What do I really believe about the afterlife? How do my beliefs make a difference in how I'm living right now?*

♦ *What things in my life seem to have a sense of "completion" about them? What things are still left undone?*

♦ *As I think about the future, what role does "preparing for my eternal destiny" play in my plans and goals?*

Realize that All Things Come to an End . . .

There is a time for everything,

and a season for every activity under heaven:
a time to be born and a time to die,
a time to plant and a time to uproot,
a time to kill and a time to heal,
a time to tear down and a time to build,
a time to weep and a time to laugh,
a time to mourn and a time to dance,
a time to scatter stones and a time to gather them,
a time to embrace and a time to refrain,
a time to search and a time to give up,
a time to keep and a time to throw away,
a time to tear and a time to mend,
a time to be silent and a time to speak,
a time to love and a time to hate,
a time for war and a time for peace. *-Ecclesiastes 3:1-8*

God Brings an End to Death and Grief Forever

I know that my Redeemer lives,
and that in the end he will stand upon the earth.

And after my skin has been destroyed,
yet in my flesh I will see God;
I myself will see him with my own eyes—
I, and not another. How my heart yearns within me! *-Job 19:25-27*

Even though I walk
through the valley of the shadow of death,
I will fear no evil, for you are with me;
your rod and your staff, they comfort me.
You prepare a table before me
in the presence of my enemies.
You anoint my head with oil; my cup overflows.
Surely goodness and love will follow me all the days of my life,
and I will dwell in the house of the LORD forever. *-Psalm 23:4-6*

For you have delivered me from death
and my feet from stumbling,
that I may walk before God in the light of life.
-Psalm 56:13

For you, O LORD, have delivered my soul from death,
my eyes from tears, my feet from stumbling. *-Psalm 116:8*

Do not be amazed at this, for a time is coming when all who are in their graves will hear his voice and come out—those who have done good will rise to live, and those who have done evil will rise to be condemned. *-John 5:28, 29*

In my Father's house are many rooms; if it were not so, I would have told you. I am going there to prepare a place for you. And if I go and prepare a place for you, I will come back and take you to be with me that you also may be where I am. *-John 14:2, 3*

I consider that our present sufferings are not worth comparing with the glory that will be revealed in us. *-Romans 8:18*

However, as it is written: "No eye has seen, no ear has heard, no mind has conceived what God has prepared for those who love him." *-I Corinthians 2:9*

For what I received I passed on to you as of first importance: that Christ died for our sins according to the Scriptures, that he was buried, that he was raised on the third day according to the Scriptures. . . .

But if it is preached that Christ has been raised from the dead, how can some of you say that there is no resurrection of the dead? If there is no resurrection of the dead, then not even Christ has been raised. And if Christ has not been raised, our preaching is useless and so is your faith. More than that, we are then found to be false witnesses about God, for we have testified about God that he raised Christ from the dead. But he did not raise him if in fact the dead are not raised.

For if the dead are not raised, then Christ has not been raised either. And if Christ has not been raised, your faith is futile; you are still in your sins. Then those also who have fallen asleep in Christ are lost. If only for this life we have hope in Christ, we are to be pitied more than all men. But Christ has indeed been raised from the dead, the firstfruits of those who have fallen asleep. . . .

Listen, I tell you a mystery: We will not all sleep, but we will all be changed— in a flash, in the twinkling of an eye, at the last trumpet. For the trumpet will sound, the dead will be raised imperishable, and we will be changed. For the perishable must clothe itself with the imperishable, and the mortal with immortality. When the perishable has been clothed with the imperishable, and the mortal with immortality, then the saying that is written will come true: "Death has been swallowed up in victory."

"Where, O death, is your victory? Where, O death, is your sting?"

-I Corinthians 15:3, 4, 12-20, 51-55

Brothers, we do not want you to be ignorant about those who fall asleep, or to grieve like the rest of men, who have no hope. We believe that Jesus died and rose again and so we believe that God will bring with Jesus those who have fallen asleep in him. According to the Lord's own word, we tell you that we who are still alive, who are left till the coming of the Lord, will certainly not precede those who have fallen asleep. For the Lord himself will come down from heaven, with a loud command, with the voice of the archangel and with the trumpet call of God, and the dead in Christ will rise first. After that, we who are still alive and are left will be caught up together with them in the clouds to meet the Lord in the air. And so we will be with the Lord forever. Therefore encourage each other with these words. *- I Thessalonians 4:13-18*

But in keeping with his promise we are looking forward to a new heaven and a new earth, the home of righteousness. *-II Peter 3:13*

Nevertheless, I have this against you: You tolerate that woman Jezebel, who calls herself a prophetess. By her teaching she misleads my servants into sexual immorality and the eating of food sacrificed to idols. *-Revelation 2:20*

After this I looked and there before me was a great multitude that no one could count, from every nation, tribe, people and language, standing before the throne and in front of the Lamb. They were wearing white robes and were holding palm branches in their hands. And they cried out in a loud voice: "Salvation belongs to our God, who sits on the throne, and to the Lamb." All the angels were standing around the throne and around the elders and the four living creatures. They fell down on their faces before the throne and worshiped God, saying: "Amen! Praise and glory and wisdom and thanks and honor and power and strength be to our God for ever and ever. Amen!"

Then one of the elders asked me, "These in white robes—who are they, and where did they come from?" I answered, "Sir, you know." And he said, "These are they who have come out of the great tribulation; they have washed their robes and made them white in the blood of the Lamb. Therefore, they are before the throne of God and serve him day and night in his temple; and he who sits on the throne will spread his tent over them. Never again will they hunger; never again will they thirst. The sun will not beat upon them, nor any scorching heat. For the Lamb at the center of the throne will be their shepherd; he will lead them to springs of living water. And God will wipe away every tear from their eyes." -*Revelation 7:9-17*

God Promises a Heavenly Home

In my Father's house are many rooms; if it were not so, I would have told you. I am going there to prepare a place for you. And if I go and prepare a place for you, I will come back and take you to be with me that you also may be where I am. *-John 14:2, 3*

Then I saw a new heaven and a new earth, for the first heaven and the first earth had passed away, and there was no longer any sea. I saw the Holy City, the new Jerusalem, coming down out of heaven from God, prepared as a bride beautifully dressed for her husband. And I heard a loud voice from the throne saying, "Now the dwelling of God is with men, and he will live with them. They will be his people, and God himself will be with them and be their God. He will wipe every tear from their eyes. There will be no more death or mourning or crying or pain, for the old order of things has passed away." *-Revelation 21:1-4*

The city was laid out like a square, as long as it was wide. He measured the city with the rod and found it to be 12,000 stadia in length, and as wide and high as it is long. He measured its wall and it was 144 cubits thick, by man's measurement, which the angel was using. The wall was made of jasper, and the city of pure gold, as pure as glass. The foundations of the city walls were decorated with every kind of precious stone. The first foundation was jasper, the second sapphire, the third chalcedony, the fourth emerald, the fifth sardonyx, the sixth carnelian, the seventh chrysolite, the eighth beryl, the ninth topaz, the tenth chrysoprase, the eleventh jacinth, and the twelfth amethyst. The twelve gates were twelve pearls, each gate made of a single pearl. The great street of the city was of pure gold, like transparent glass.

I did not see a temple in the city, because the Lord God Almighty and the Lamb are its temple. The city does not need the sun or the moon to shine on it, for the glory of God gives it light, and the Lamb is its lamp. The nations will walk by its light, and the kings of the earth will bring their splendor into it. On no day will its gates ever be shut, for there will be no night there. The glory and honor of the nations will be brought into it. Nothing impure will ever enter it, nor will anyone who does what is shameful or deceitful, but only those whose names are written in the Lamb's book of life.

-Revelation 21:16-27

God Makes Us Heirs to a Crown

Everyone who competes in the games goes into strict training. They do it to get a crown that will not last; but we do it to get a crown that will last forever. *-I Corinthians 9:25*

Now there is in store for me the crown of righteousness, which the Lord, the righteous Judge, will award to me on that day—and not only to me, but also to all who have longed for his appearing. *-II Timothy 4:8*

Blessed is the man who perseveres under trial, because when he has stood the test, he will receive the crown of life that God has promised to those who love him. *-James 1:12*

And when the Chief Shepherd appears, you will receive the crown of glory that will never fade away. *-1 Peter 5:4*

Do not be afraid of what you are about to suffer. I tell you, the devil will put some of you in prison to test you, and you will suffer persecution for ten days. Be faithful, even to the point of death, and I will give you the crown of life. *-Revelation 2:10*

God Has Promised Spiritual Blessing
I am the LORD your God,
who brought you up out of Egypt.
Open wide your mouth and I will fill it. *-Psalm 81:10*

Blessed are those whose strength is in you,
who have set their hearts on pilgrimage. *-Psalm 84:5*

Then your light will break forth like the dawn,
and your healing will quickly appear;
then your righteousness will go before you,
and the glory of the LORD will be your rear guard.
Then you will call, and the LORD will answer;
you will cry for help, and he will say: Here am I.
"If you do away with the yoke of oppression,
with the pointing finger and malicious talk,
and if you spend yourselves in behalf of the hungry
and satisfy the needs of the oppressed,
then your light will rise in the darkness,
and your night will become like the noonday.
The LORD will guide you always;
he will satisfy your needs in a sun-scorched land
and will strengthen your frame.
You will be like a well-watered garden,
like a spring whose waters never fail. *-Isaiah 58:8-11*

"They will come and shout for joy on the heights of Zion;

they will rejoice in the bounty of the LORD—
the grain, the new wine and the oil,
the young of the flocks and herds.
They will be like a well-watered garden,
and they will sorrow no more.
Then maidens will dance and be glad,
young men and old as well.
I will turn their mourning into gladness;
I will give them comfort and joy instead of sorrow.
I will satisfy the priests with abundance,
and my people will be filled with my bounty," declares the LORD.

-Jeremiah 31:12-14

So Look to the Future with Hope

I tell you the truth, you will weep and mourn while the world rejoices.
You will grieve, but your grief will turn to joy. *-John 16:20*

So do not throw away your confidence; it will be richly rewarded. You need to persevere
so that when you have done the will of God, you will receive what he has promised. For

in just a very little while, "He who is coming will come and will not delay. But my right-eous one will live by faith. And if he shrinks back, I will not be pleased with him."

-Hebrews 10:35-38

Therefore, since we are surrounded by such a great cloud of witnesses, let us throw off everything that hinders and the sin that so easily entangles, and let us run with perseverance the race marked out for us. Let us fix our eyes on Jesus, the author and perfecter of our faith, who for the joy set before him endured the cross, scorning its shame, and sat down at the right hand of the throne of God. *-Hebrews 12:1, 2*

> If you devote your heart to him
> and stretch out your hands to him,
> if you put away the sin that is in your hand
> and allow no evil to dwell in your tent,
> then you will lift up your face without shame;
> you will stand firm and without fear.
> You will surely forget your trouble,
> recalling it only as waters gone by.
> Life will be brighter than noonday,

and darkness will become like morning.
You will be secure, because there is hope;
you will look about you and take your rest in safety.
You will lie down, with no one to make you afraid,
and many will court your favor. *-Job 11:13-19*

For his anger lasts only a moment,
but his favor lasts a lifetime;
weeping may remain for a night,
but rejoicing comes in the morning. *-Psalm 30:5*

Though he brings grief,
he will show compassion,
so great is his unfailing love. *-Lamentations 3:32*

FOR PERSONAL PRAYER:

Lord, You hold my future in the palm of Your hand. I need more faith, daily, that all Your plans for me spring from Your love and concern for my good. Until the day you take me home. Amen.